Literacy Through Play

GRETCHEN OWOCKI

Foreword by Sue Bredekamp

HEINEMANN

Portsmouth, NH

Heinemann
A division of Reed Elsevier Inc.
361 Hanover Street
Portsmouth, NH 03801-3912
http://www.heinemann.com

Offices and agents throughout the world

© 1999 by Gretchen Owocki

Library of Congress Cataloging-in-Publication Data
Owocki, Gretchen.
     Literacy through play / Gretchen Owocki ; foreword by Sue Bredekamp ; [editor, Lois Bridges].
        p.   cm.
     Includes bibliographical references.
     ISBN 0-325-00127-8 (alk. paper)
     1. Language arts (Early childhood).   2. Play.   3. Language acquisition.   4. Classroom learning centers.   I. Bridges, Lois.
     II. Title.
     LB1139.5.L35086   1999
     372.6 — dc21   98-54827
                                                             CIP

Editor: Lois Bridges
Production: Vicki Kasabian
Cover design: Jenny Jensen Greenleaf
Manufacturing: Louise Richardson

Printed in the United States of America on acid-free paper
07 06 05   DA   11 12 13 14

To David Owocki

Contents

Foreword

When my sister and I were little girls, we liked nothing better than to drag out our plastic dollhouse furniture and little people, as we called the movable figures, and play for hours. Much too confining, the dollhouse itself was employed rarely. Instead, we spread the furniture into elaborate, ever-changing configurations. Then, drawing on our limited life experience, which was greatly supplemented by my mother's soap operas, we played and played. To initiate this great fun, we had a shared signal. One of us would excitedly, almost conspiratorially say to the other, "Do you want to tell a story?"

Reading Gretchen Owocki's delightful book, *Literacy Through Play*, brought back these and other childhood memories for me. Because Owocki describes the role of play in literacy learning beyond the preschool years, a topic that is usually neglected, I was also reminded of playing with other children in my 1950s neighborhood. In our middle-class suburban enclave, our mothers were all stay-at-home but they didn't see themselves as our first teachers. For example, when at age five, I asked my mother to help me write my name, she said no, my teacher would do that when I went to school. Instead, she sent us out to play where we stayed virtually all day constructing forts, pirate ships, and other elaborate schemes that provided highly valuable but rare opportunities for conversation between the younger and older kids. The older kids also provided the little ones with terrific instruction in phonemic awareness as they tried to trick us into saying bad words. "It rhymes with Sam," they'd challenge us.

The point of these reminiscences is not to idealize the past, but to emphasize that the underlying principles of child development and learning apply in different, ever-changing social and cultural contexts. Today's preschoolers are likely to be found in formal educational settings outside the home, but play is still the most appropriate context for development and learning. It's also the preferred one. For example, when Nancy Wiltz and Elisa Klein from the University of Maryland asked 122 four-year-olds what they like to do at school, 98 percent answered play and play activities. If, as Owocki and many others have found through research, play is such an effective vehicle for early literacy learning, let's start listening to the children and using play to teach. This book provides a clear path for teachers to begin or expand that work.

Literacy Through Play is a resource for teachers who are learning to use play as a medium for facilitating literacy in preschool, kindergarten, and first-grade classrooms. Teachers who are just beginning to connect literacy and play will appreciate the straightforward theoretical rationale for using play in the classroom, as well as the numerous practical ideas of teaching through play, developing the play environment, assessing children's literacy knowledge as they play, implementing developmentally appropriate practice, and collaborating with families.

My sister and I grew up, at least chronologically speaking. We are very different people, but we are surprisingly similar in two ways. We are voracious readers by choice, and we are writers by profession, she a novelist and I an expository writer. Perhaps because I see my own life and the lives of so many children I've known in Gretchen Owocki's book, I find it beautiful. Do you want to tell a story? Let's play!

Sue Bredekamp, Ph.D.
NAEYC Director of Professional Development

Acknowledgments

I wish to thank Christine Eaton, Trish Hill, and Curt Kiwak for welcoming me into their classrooms, for allowing me to write about their work, and above all, for taking teaching to its greatest heights. I also wish to thank the many other teachers (particularly in Tucson, Arizona) whose classrooms I have visited and who have helped me to understand the ins and outs of their wonderful work with children.

Many thanks to all the children whose language and ideas are included in this book. I am grateful to their families for their interest and support.

A special thanks to Suzanne Arquette, Sally Edgerton, Susie Emond, and Heather Mlsna for responding to early drafts of this book, for their encouragement, and, especially, for their friendship.

Finally, I wish to thank Yetta Goodman for her insight and counsel as I conducted the research that led to this book.

1

Play and Developmentally Appropriate Practices

C hildren explore multiple worlds and perspectives as they move in and out of their play. As astronauts and space travelers, they puzzle over the future; as dinosaurs and princesses, they unearth the past. As weather reporters and restaurant workers, they make sense of reality; as monsters and gremlins, they make sense of the unreal. As children move through their multiple play worlds, they explore and elaborate on their understandings of many things—including written language:

> Marco is pointing at a map with a wooden cylinder. "Ninety degrees today," he says in a formal tone. "Tucson was just a sunny day. 'Mockie-aleena' was just a floody day. Mexico wasn't not floody. Right here was real floody. Not floods right here, and right here, and right here, too."

Do you think that Marco has seen a weather report on television? My bet is that he has. Play gives him the opportunity to explore his understanding of a weather report and of the kind of language and props that a weather reporter uses. A wonderful by-product of this event is that he explores a piece of written language—a map—perhaps using it in a way that he has not used it before. Play provides Marco with the opportunity to explore and elaborate on his understandings of his world and the written language that is a part of that world. Let's look at another example:

> Piper and her aunt are quietly waiting for the others to awaken. There will be seven for breakfast. "Maybe we could have a restaurant," suggests the aunt. Piper finds a pencil and paper and sits on the couch to make a menu. "I'm doing it in cursive," she announces, "what are we having?" As the aunt names the foods, Piper writes an *M* followed by squiggly lines for *milk*; a *G*

followed by squiggles for *grape* juice; a *B* and squiggles for *bagels;* a *T* for *toast;* a *G* for *grapes;* an *O* for *orange juice;* an *S* for *cereal;* and a *B* for *bananas* (Figure 1–1).

Like Marco, Piper is exploring her world through play. It is clear that she knows what a menu is, and knows the kind of information it should contain. Her play gives her an opportunity to investigate that knowledge and also to try out some things she hasn't tried before: she creates a menu, makes it available to customers, and sees how they use it to inform themselves. Because Piper lives in a literacy-rich world, written language is a part of what she explores through her play. Her use of initial consonants followed by invented cursive strings serves her purpose as a restaurant worker quite nicely. She sees that her family members can use the clues she provides to guess what they might eat for breakfast. As with Marco, written language is included in the many things Piper explores through play. Let's look at one more example of a child exploring written language through play.

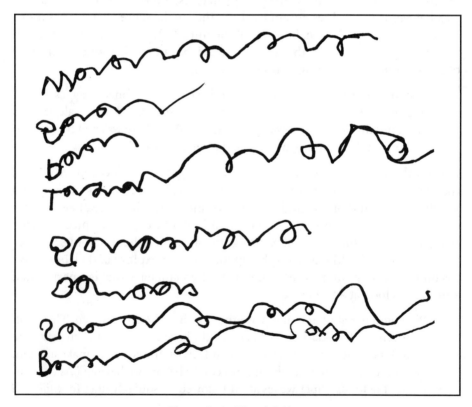

Figure 1–1. Piper's Menu

Harry and his friends are playing in Jurassic Park, traveling amidst a world full of dangerous dinosaurs. Harry goes to the writing table, writes a string of letters, draws a box around what he has written, and reads aloud: "Beware of dinosaurs in this country. They could hurt you very badly" (Figure 1–2). He tells his friends what the sign says.

Somewhere, either in a book, on film, or through play, Harry has discovered that dinosaurs had characteristics that made them potentially dangerous to live with. How they moved, what they ate, and how they behaved are thoroughly explored in his play. The children's dinosaur play theme also provides a meaningful context for the use of written language. Harry creates a warning sign for the humans who are fearfully traveling through the park.

Children expand their knowledge of the world through play. Expanding their knowledge about written language is no different. Because Marco, Piper, and Harry live in a print-filled society, it is not surprising that they frequently bring reading and writing into their play. Using print is important because becoming literate begins with understanding the various ways in which written language is used—the various *functions* it serves (Goodman 1996; McGee and Richgels 1996; Taylor 1983). As children use written language in their play, they discover many of its features—the formation of letters, the spellings of words, the meanings of words, and how punctuation works.

Play is like a gold mine in its potential for facilitating literacy. First, it provides lots of clues for sorting out aspects of written language. For example, play might help children to figure out what an unfamiliar sign means, how a list is used, what a map is for, or what a word says. Children's play is about what is familiar to them, so play typically provides a meaningful context for children to construct new knowledge and for teachers to facilitate this construction. Second, play provides a safe environment for risk taking. Children can try out new ideas without worrying about the consequences. For example, Piper can

Figure 1–2. Harry's Warning Sign

try out a list of words on her family and not worry about whether they will be able to read it. Marco can try out creative uses of language and not worry about whether he will be understood. Children have to take risks to learn. It is how they build new knowledge (Harste, Burke, and Woodward 1981).

As children use print and negotiate its structures, meanings, and purposes in their play, they construct necessary knowledge for real-life reading and writing. As a teacher, you can facilitate this construction by purposefully watching for and capitalizing on teachable moments. Within the context of play with miniature cars, you might help a child see the need for a Wrong Way sign and then help the child to construct a spelling for these words. Within the context of hospital play, you might help a group of children develop a chart to record which patients have been examined and given medication. For an older child playing in a "newsroom," you might assist with the format for writing an article, a comic strip, a recipe, or an advertisement. As you work with children in these ways, you are facilitating their understandings about written language. Facilitation implies providing a temporary framework for knowledge construction (Cazden 1983) as it is meaningful to the child—the teachable moment.

Watching for teachable moments during play makes sense developmentally because it helps you provide instruction that is directly connected to children's current understandings. If it is our goal is to help children build on their current understandings at individualized paces, then this could be called a *developmentally appropriate practice.*

BACKGROUND ON THE BOOK

This book is for teachers who wish to explore developmentally appropriate practices in literacy instruction. The major focus is on facilitating literacy through play. Most of the examples and ideas come from the children and colleagues whose classrooms I have visited and studied over the past five years. Many come from my own preschool, kindergarten, and first-grade teaching experiences.

I became interested in literacy and play fifteen years ago as an aide in a kindergarten classroom. The teacher in that classroom valued play and provided many opportunities for her children to explore their worlds through play. She also had a special interest in teaching children to read, and I picked up on her enthusiasm for both.

In my own classrooms I, too, offered many opportunities for play and became enchanted by the worlds my children created and by the unique insights they demonstrated while playing. It made sense for me to pursue graduate studies in the areas of literacy and play; I wanted to learn more about literacy, more about play, and more about connecting the two. At the University of Arizona, I conducted an eighteen-month study on how teachers facilitate literacy through play, and, as an assistant professor of Literacy and Early Childhood Education at a small university in Michigan, I have continued this line of inquiry in early childhood classrooms. As you read, you will meet some of the teachers with whom I have worked and be witness to the creative ways in which they use play as a medium for facilitating literacy. This book is a culmination of research, including my own, about the ways in which holistic, developmentally appropriate practices are effectively implemented in classrooms.

TO THINK ABOUT AS YOU READ

The concept of using play as developmentally appropriate instruction remains unclear to many teachers. Some wonder how to effectively use play in their classrooms (Schrader 1991). Others are uncertain about how to meet literacy-related curricular goals and objectives through play. Many want to know more about designing a physical environment for play (Roskos et al. 1995). Even teachers who are comfortable using play and who understand its potential for facilitating learning worry that children will be unprepared for standardized tests or future academic experiences. Recent media reports criticizing holistic styles of teaching have many wondering whether developing a child-centered philosophy for teaching is worthwhile.

This book discusses how children develop literacy and how teachers in early childhood classrooms use play and other child-centered experiences to facilitate literacy development. It demonstrates a theoretical rationale for using play to teach and includes ideas for setting up the play environment, planning for play, and using play to facilitate literacy in developmentally appropriate ways. The current political firestorm over reading, phonics, or spelling has teachers concerned that children in holistic or developmentally appropriate classrooms will not develop the ability to read, write, and spell conventionally. This book will assuage those concerns. If the Back-to-Basics movement has led you to question whether basic literacy skills are taught in developmentally appropriate classrooms, this book not only will confirm for you that they are, but also will give you usable ideas for teaching the "basics" in developmentally appropriate ways. I raise this controversial issue because I want you to decide for yourself whether children in developmentally appropriate classrooms are learning the conventions of written language and are developing strategies used by successful readers and writers.

DEVELOPMENTALLY APPROPRIATE PRACTICE

The National Association for the Education of Young Children (NAEYC) defines a *developmentally appropriate practice* as one that is based on decision making using three kinds of knowledge: (1) knowledge about development and learning; (2) knowledge about individual children; and (3) knowledge about children's sociocultural contexts for living and growing (Bredekamp and Copple 1997). As you teach through play, your knowledge in these areas guides your instructional decision making.

Knowledge About Development and Learning

Knowledge about development and learning involves *understanding children's typical patterns of growth*. What we know about children's development is that it "occurs in a relatively orderly sequence, with later abilities, skills, and knowledge building on those already acquired" (Bredekamp and Copple 1997, 10). Although variation is expected, similarities have been observed in the ways children develop. For example, many children at an early age will pretend to drink from a toy cup. It is not until later that they pretend to drink from, say, a cylindrical block. Play researchers have observed that younger children typically play with toys in a direct way while older children develop the ability to use them symbolically. Similarly, many children invent spellings using mostly consonants at first. It is not until later that they begin to add vowels. Knowledge about typical patterns of children's play and literacy development helps teachers make predictions about where children are likely to go next in their thinking. Anticipating children's next steps makes it possible to plan meaningful and challenging instruction. For example, if you know that young children need realistic objects in order to pretend, you make sure that they have realistic props for play.

Knowledge About Individual Children

The second kind of knowledge that early childhood teachers use to inform their decision making involves *understanding individual children's strengths, needs, and interests*. Although general patterns of development remain similar from child to child, each child develops a unique cognitive configuration because of personal experiences and distinctive ways of reflecting on these experiences (Bowman 1994). Learning is a process of doing and reflecting on doing (Adelman 1992). No two children will "do" or reflect on doing in just the same way. By the time they enter school, children have vastly different ways of approaching learning, they have different talents, interests, and abilities, and they have unique preferences and tastes. Early childhood teachers learn everything they can about particular children, always adapting their instruction to respond to particular strengths, interests, and needs. Teaming up with families and observing play are good ways to develop knowledge about individual children's strengths, needs, and interests. Play is a good time to respond to the individual because it provides an arena for children to demonstrate their interests, and through them, their strengths.

Knowledge About Children's Sociocultural Contexts

The third kind of knowledge that is necessary for implementing developmentally appropriate practice involves *understanding children's sociocultural contexts for living and growing.* As children move through their early childhood years, they develop a set of rules and expectations for behavior, many of which are shared by other members of the cultural groups to which they belong. Like any kind of knowledge, sociocultural knowledge is a part of children's development. Elements of children's sociocultural knowledge may be reflected in the ways they use language, in their nonverbal communication, in their preferred approaches to learning, and in their styles of interacting with people.

Think about what this means in a school setting. While one child may be accustomed to being told to "sit down," another may be more accustomed to being asked "Would you like to come and join us?" While for one child, respect may be shown by looking someone in the eyes, for another it may be shown by averting the eyes. Some children are comfortable standing and sitting close to others; some prefer a bit of distance. While certain children are comfortable being touched on the arm or shoulder, others withdraw from touch. Elements of cultural knowledge are reflected in how children organize their time, how they interact socially, what they choose to wear, what and when they eat, how they worship, and how they respond to major life events, celebrations, and changes (Bredekamp and Copple 1997). It is the responsibility of the teacher to learn about the sociocultural contexts in which children live and grow and to use that information as a resource for teaching.

Both play and collaboration with families provide a window into children's cultural understandings. The observation and assessment techniques discussed in Chapter 5 can help you develop insights into children's sociocultural contexts for living and growing. Chapters 5 and 6 center around developing a meaningful environment for literacy through play that is responsive to children's typical patterns of development, to their individual patterns, and to their sociocultural contexts for living and growing.

PLAY AND ITS RELATIONSHIP TO DEVELOPMENT

Children actively explore their worlds. As we saw at the beginning of the chapter, play provides an arena for this exploration. But what is play, exactly? One thing is clear: play is more easily recognized than it is defined (Linder 1993). Defining play in terms of its developmental characteristics, or the sequence in which it typically unfolds as children move through the early childhood years, makes it possible to look at play and its relationship to cognitive and social development.

Play and Cognitive Development

Play researchers (Johnson, Christie, and Yawkey 1987; Piaget 1962; Van Hoorn et al. 1993) have observed that children's play behaviors become more complex and abstract as they progress through early childhood. This progression can be illustrated by exploring three kinds of play, which develop roughly in sequence: exploratory, constructive, and dramatic.

Exploratory Play

> Demetrius pulls a piece of play dough from the storage container. He chooses a hammer from the basket on the table and begins to pound the play dough over and over. When it is flat, he borrows a rolling pin from Nathan, and rolls and rolls.

In *exploratory play* children do things over and over to experience the joy of having mastered something new and to affirm for themselves their newly acquired abilities (Piaget and Inhelder 1969). They pound and knead play dough, sift and pat sand, or run their fingers through water because they enjoy the effects of these actions and because it feels good to be capable. *Exploratory play* is different from *exploration*. In exploration, children engage in the same kinds of repetitive actions, but with a different goal. In exploration, the child's goal is to discover properties of objects or materials:

> Brian is dabbing yellow paint onto a blue piece of paper. The result is a light shade of green. "You know what? This looks like yellow, but it's actually green," he tells his teacher, Pete, as he continues to dab the paint. Pete responds, "Well, what color do you get when you mix blue and yellow?" Brian's face shows his dawning understanding: "Green!"

Is Brian playing (enjoying the feel and look of what he is doing) or is he exploring (attempting to discover the properties of the colors he is using)? I would guess that he is doing a bit of both, but it is hard to tell. The distinction between exploration and exploratory play is fuzzy (McCall 1979). First, who can say what a child's goals are at any given time? Second, children frequently move back and forth between exploration and exploratory play, making it even harder to tell them apart. The good news is that you need not struggle extensively to distinguish between the two. Both help children to make discoveries about their physical worlds. However, it doesn't hurt to reflect on whether your children are going beyond exploration in their efforts. If they don't go beyond exploration, it could be that the materials are too difficult to use or that they are unsure about how to use them.

Exploratory play predominates between birth and age two, but remains important throughout the early childhood years. In fact, it remains important throughout adulthood. Think about how you, as an adult, might enjoy bouncing on a trampoline just for the sake of bouncing. It's fun and it feels good. You might even experiment with maneuvers, repeating them for the mere pleasure they bring. Do you play with bubbles in the bath? Do you doodle on paper? Do you enjoy playing with a helium-filled balloon? Gardening is a hobby I enjoy. When I bring a tray full of different perennials home from the greenhouse, I start out in an exploratory mode. I examine the different textures of the petals and leaves because I want to learn about their properties. I know that certain kinds of flowers will do well in certain parts of my yard. I also enjoy the feel, the fragrance, and the appearance of the flowers. If the leaves are fuzzy, I stroke them; if they are succulent, I give them a squeeze. If the fragrance is nice, I sniff. Sometimes I line up the flowers, moving them this way and that to see which colors look good together. If two colors are particularly dazzling together, I spend some time enjoying their splendor. My exploration is important to me not only because it brings pleasure, but also because it helps me to develop as a gardener. I continually reflect on which kinds of plants need more water, which do well in shade, which draw garden pests, which are the most fragrant, which bloom all summer, and which my dogs will easily crush. As I continue to explore and reflect, I develop new and progressively more complex insights into effective gardening. If I had to listen to someone tell me all of this, or if I could only read it in a book, I don't think I would understand so well.

Children are the same way. They "are more likely to understand and remember relationships, concepts and strategies that they acquire through firsthand, meaningful experience" (Bredekamp and Copple 1997, 114). Developmentally appropriate practice suggests that children need as many firsthand experiences as possible and that teachers can facilitate their thinking as they engage in these experiences, as Pete did with Brian in the paint-dabbing vignette. Throughout the early childhood years—and beyond—opportunities for exploratory activity remain important both for development and for the pleasure they bring. Both exploratory play and exploration remain essential parts of an early childhood curriculum (Van Hoorn et al. 1993).

Constructive Play

In *constructive play* children begin to use objects or materials to create a *representation* of something. For example, children might use a row of large blocks to represent a road and use small blocks to represent cars. Blocks are mentally transformed into something else. Constructive play becomes increasingly more complex over time. Early on children may stack a few blocks to make a tower; later, children build complex structures such as zoos, parks, castles, and garages (Johnson, Christie, and Yawkey 1987).

Constructive play increases in frequency as children move from toddlerhood into the preschool years, but does not replace exploratory play. In fact, it is typical for children of all ages to physically explore materials, especially if they are unfamiliar, before using them to build or pretend. You probably observe this when you bring something new to your classroom or when you set up a new sand, water, or rice table; all the children want to get their hands on the new materials to explore. Only later do they move into a constructive or pretend mode of play.

Dramatic Play

Constructive play provides a natural link to *dramatic play,* in which children use objects, actions, and language to create imaginary roles and situations (Van Hoorn et al. 1993). Let's look at an example from Curt Kiwak and Trish Hill's preschool classroom: One day the children came in from outdoors saying that they wanted to play "eagle." Curt found a basket full of plastic eggs and after holding the eggs and discussing their colors, the children began to search for material to build nests. Colin and Karla crinkled paper to build nests and then placed their eggs in the nests to hatch. Curt, needing to remove himself from the play, put his egg under a lamb puppet and told the children that the lamb was going to baby-sit. Colin followed these actions and shared the use of the lamb as a baby-sitter.

Notice how children's play becomes more complex as they move from exploration to construction to dramatic play. At first, they explored the physical properties of objects; then they used objects to represent something. Let's look at an another example of four- and five-year-olds engaged in dramatic play. As you read the example, think about the symbolic representation that is taking place. Again, we go to Curt and Trish's classroom:

> Colin, Bowen, Todd, and Diego have set up a space station in the home-living area. Colin is at a computer keyboard, pressing the keys as he counts

down. "Ten . . . nine . . . eight . . . seven . . . five—I mean, ten . . . nine . . . eight . . . seven . . . six . . . five . . . four . . . three . . . two . . . one. It's going to be a hard landing. We're going to blast off." Colin makes noises that sound like a blastoff. Todd asks, "What about your seat belt?" Colin pretends to buckle on a seat belt. Todd, Bowen, and Diego start to do the same. "No," Colin says, "you don't need them any more. We're already in space."

Dramatic play is characterized by the mental transformation of objects, actions, and situations. The children mentally transform an object—an old keyboard—into a control panel for guiding the spaceship. They also mentally transform actions. Their bouncing up and down represents being shaken by the ship and their hand gestures represent the donning of seat belts. Together, the children have created an imaginative situation—they are astronauts traveling in space.

Does the ability to play in this way have something to do with written language development? You bet it does! As children at play engage in mental transformations, they develop the capacity to work with a wide range of abstractions, including alphabetic symbols. Vygotsky (1978) explains that when children transform the meaning of objects or actions they change a usual meaning into something imaginary. They take a concrete object and interpret it in an abstract way. In order to be able to read and write, children must do something similar. They must understand that written symbols—those black marks on paper—carry meaning. The symbols (letters) are more than just marks on a page—they represent something. They can be sounds and words; they are used to write names, label objects, tell stories, and give information. Children who play symbolically get good at using symbols and develop the ability to mentally manipulate them. While early on, they need the actual object to engage in the transformation, as they become more advanced, a mental representation suffices (Vygotsky 1978).

When children are just beginning to engage in symbolic play, they typically stick to themes that are "close to home." For example, two-year-old Chloe put some spools into a bowl and pretended to eat them. She gave a spool to her teacher, Curt, telling him "It's a little bit like juicy, like milk, like strawberry." Chloe has mentally transformed one object into another—a spool is a symbol for tasty food. Two- and three-year-olds often act out themes and situations that are close to those which they have actually experienced. They pretend to eat, to cook food, to sleep, and to take care of dolls. They go grocery shopping, driving in a car, or visiting at grandma's house. As they gain experience in the world, their themes for play expand, and they explore the diverse perspectives and life experiences of the members of their wider sociocultural environments. This is important to keep in mind as you develop the play environment. Children who are moving into symbolic forms of play benefit from concrete, close-to-home play props.

Developmentally Sensitive Teaching

Understanding that there is a relative sequence for the development of play helps teachers know what to expect from children and how to help them grow. When talking about a progression through stages of play we have to keep in mind that this progression is not the same for any two children and is by no means cut in stone. These stages have been identified as a typical course of development for many children. They reflect not only maturation, but also life experiences, experience with play, and the conceptual understandings developed so far. At various times and for various reasons, children go back and forth between the stages. This is perfectly natural and is *to be expected*. Children do not abandon early forms of play once later forms have been mastered. Instead, they continually incorporate what they can do into new play events. The stages simply provide a developmental framework that gives teachers a general idea of what to expect from children, and where they may go next in their thinking. Thinking in this way enables you to provide appropriate materials and to support children in challenging and sensitive ways.

Play and Social Development

Mildred Parten (1932) studied the connections between children's play and social development. She identified four levels of play that children develop as they move through the early childhood years: solitary, parallel, associative, and cooperative. Parten established these categories after observing that children's play becomes more interactive over time. However, one form of play does not replace previous forms once it develops; rather, children move back and forth among the levels throughout the early childhood years (Monighan-Nourot et al. 1987). As with any kind of development, we expect children to vary in their preferred ways of playing. Some children prefer to play alone, while others enjoy engaging in group play. Most of the children you will meet in this book have developed the ability to engage in associative and cooperative play (which Parten observed to emerge between the ages of three and a half and four and a half), and move comfortably back and forth among the levels.

Solitary Play

Solitary play is characterized by children engaging in independent activity. For example, Tanya sits by herself near a basket full of toy dinosaurs. She lines up three dinosaurs and places three little plates in front of them. Tanya is playing by herself and is not noticeably influenced by any of the activity around her. Tanya is engaged in solitary play. Although solitary play is an early form of play, it continues to remain important throughout the early childhood years.

Parallel Play

In *parallel play* children use similar toys and/or engage in similar activities, but do not play together. Picture Jesusita sitting on the rug near Tanya, pulling a handful of dinosaurs from the basket. She, too, places the dinosaurs in a row. Children engaged in parallel play notice what others are doing, often getting ideas for their own play. They may use parallel play as a means of working their way into an existing play situation or to draw others into their play. They may even use it as a way of moving out of a play situation.

Associative Play

Associative play is characterized by children engaging in similar, somewhat organized activity. Children may talk about what they or others are doing, share toys, and ask each other questions. Jesusita asks Tanya, "Can I have some of those plates? My dinosaurs are eating grass." In associative play, children do not engage in joint efforts toward an end product such as carrying out a game or dramatizing a situation, but they do talk with others about play-related issues.

Cooperative Play

Cooperative play involves two or more children engaging in a joint effort toward a common purpose. Players take on different responsibilities or roles to jointly negotiate and organize their play themes. For example, Tanya gets a box of cardboard puzzle pieces from the shelf. The puzzle pieces are shaped like bread, peanut butter, and jelly. "Let's make peanut butter and jelly sandwiches." She makes several sandwiches while Jesusita lines up dinosaurs and plates. Together, they feed the dinosaurs. Cooperative play takes its shape from the contributions made by all of the players.

Developmentally Sensitive Teaching

Using play to teach in a way that make sense developmentally involves keeping in mind typical patterns of social development. Young children see the world primarily from their own perspectives. Piaget called it *egocentrism.* As they get older and more experienced with play, they develop the ability to recognize and understand the perspectives of others. With their developing ability to take the perspectives of others, children become competent cooperative players. You would expect, provided they have had many opportunities to play, that a group of five-year-olds would be more adept playing cooperatively than a group of four-year-olds. Therefore, it would make sense to provide a different kind of support for these two groups. First-grade teacher Christine

Eaton expects her six- and seven-year-old students to play together cooperatively with very little adult support—although, of course, it doesn't always
work out that way (see Chapter 2).

Using play to teach in a developmentally appropriate way also involves
observing how particular children play. Try to become aware of what each
child does well in play and to determine areas in which individual children
may need your support in playing socially. Children who are emerging into associative and cooperative play will benefit from play props and themes that
suggest social interaction, but they may need your encouragement and support as they interact. For example, a post office offers more interactive possibilities than, say, a puzzle. A number of roles are needed, and children need to
talk with one another to make the play theme go. You can support children's
associative and cooperative play by modeling play behaviors (write a letter;
put it in an envelope; take it to the post office; say that you would like to mail
it; purchase a stamp). Noted play researcher Jerome Bruner (1983) has found
that children who participate in a teacher-supported intellectual activity during some period of the day play later in a more elaborate way. He suggests that
teachers and children playing together serves as a model for spontaneous,
child-initiated play at a later time.

Be sure to model adult *scripts* too: "Good morning. Do you sell stamps?
How much do they cost? Thanks. Have a great day!" Scripts are "sets of
actions and language that are conventionally used in a range of situations"
(Bredekamp and Copple 1997, 107), such as mailing a letter at the post office
or talking on the telephone. As you model scripts, it is important to base your
modeling on the knowledge and understandings children have demonstrated.
Children will employ what they have learned from modeled play only when it
is not too far beyond what they can do on their own (O'Reilly and Bornstein
1993). The important goal is not to imitate adults, but to generalize beyond
the situation in which instruction was provided (Cazden 1983).

You can also support children by helping them to interact with one another in imaginative situations. Watch for teachable moments in which a scaffold might be appropriate: "Ashley, ask Tina if you can mail the letter"; "Tina,
tell Ashley that she needs a stamp"; "Tina, it looks like you have another customer." "[M]odeling must build on what the child initiates and has a desire
to master" (Linder 1993, 109).

Keep in mind that children's personal histories and cultural experiences
will affect their ways of interacting socially during play. A child who is just
learning the language of his classmates may not have the vocabulary, or
scripts, for play using the new language. A child with a disability affecting
speech production may know the scripts, but be unable to articulate them in
a way that seems timely to the other children. A child who has not been to a

veterinary clinic is not likely to have the scripts for veterinarian play. Children in any classroom will have unique conversational styles, nonverbal behaviors, and turn-taking behaviors. They will differ in their expectations for the play behaviors of others, and in the experiences they have had with talk and play. All of these traits will influence their ways of talking and playing socially at school. To respond to children's diversity in a developmentally appropriate way involves continually thinking and learning about their typical patterns of development, their individual patterns of development, and their socio-cultural experiences, and using this knowledge to inform your teaching.

2

A Glimpse into Two Early Childhood Classrooms

Amy is making an elephant out of play dough. It has a very long nose and spirals for ears.

Karla: [*with laughter in her voice*] Is that how elephants really look, Amy?

Amy: Yeah. That's how they really look.

Aster: [*laughing*] No they don't, Amy!

Amy: [*teasing*] Yes, they have those twirls on their head. I've seen them before.

Aster: [*playing along*] Ohhhh, yeah.

Amy: Here, elephant is all finished. There's your elephant, all fixed up.

Aster laughs.

Amy: That's not an elephant. They don't look like that. I'll make a real elephant this time, okay? This elephant is going to be just perfect for you. This elephant is going to be perfect.

Karla: This elephant is going to be perfect.

Amy: Now I'm making the mouth.

Aster: Oh, neat pouth.

Amy: Now I'm making the elephant.

Aster: Oh, neat pelephant.

A VISIT TO A PRESCHOOL CLASSROOM

Under One Sun Desert School is situated in a quiet neighborhood in central Tucson. Trish Hill and Curt Kiwak are the head teachers. One other teacher is employed part-time, but works only in the late afternoons. The children at the

16

school range in age from two through six; all are members of the same class-room. Kindergartners join the preschoolers every afternoon, after attending public schools. Twelve to fifteen children are typically present. In the after-noon, Curt takes primary responsibility for the teaching while Trish moves to another room with children who need to nap. Trish and Curt feel that it is im-portant to maintain the quality of the morning program in the afternoon. They have observed a structured morning program in other preschools fol-lowed by a mandatory rest time for all of the children, and then "baby-sitting" (as opposed to informed teaching) in the afternoon. At Under One Sun, the morning and afternoon programs look much the same.

A Developmentally Appropriate Setting

Patti has had a special treat today. Her mother picked her up from school and took her out to lunch. When they return to the school, Patti stops on the side-walk just outside the door. "I don't want to go to school. I don't want you to leave. Mommy, don't go to work." Patti begins to cry. Her mother gently picks her up and carries her inside.

What do Patti and her mother see and feel as they walk into this de-velopmentally appropriate classroom? Just inside the door is a home-living center. It is stocked with dress-up clothing, small furniture, play foods, food packages, and a variety of literacy materials. Three of Patti's friends are play-ing in the home-living center. Aster is talking on the telephone while looking at a menu. "One pepperoni, one cheese," she says into the phone. Angie, too, has a telephone at her ear. She is writing as she talks. "Could we have a plain cheese, a plain pepperoni, and a sausage with pepperoni and cheese? It will take a half hour? Okay, bye." Tia is setting the table with plates and cups. She puts some play food inside a flat box labeled "Pizza."

Patti stops crying, just a bit, and with wide eyes, watches her friends. Curt had been sitting on the floor, observing their play, but now has given Patti's arm a squeeze and is talking with her mother. Patti seems to relax a little. She turns to rest her head on her mother's shoulder. She is now facing a large wooden climber with a loft on top.

The climber serves as anything from castle to rocket ship to haunted house to hospital—whatever the children decide or whatever the teachers de-cide based on themes they have noticed in the children's play. At group story time, the climber is an escape zone for children who would rather read by themselves or with friends. Right now, Bowen and Diego are sitting atop the climber, reading a book and talking about its pictures. They have chosen a favorite, easy to find because it is always on the bookshelf just next to the climber.

Patti listens momentarily to Bowen and Diego as they talk about the book. She stretches her neck a little, trying to see the pictures. Her mother follows Curt further into the classroom. Patti and her mother walk by Chloe, who is sitting at a table wearing headphones, listening to a story as she turns through the pages of a book. Written instructions for using the recorder are hanging on the wall in front of Chloe. Various signs, calendars, schedules, and samples of children's art and writing are hanging on the walls as well.

Patti's mother notices the snack schedule and points out to Patti that the children will be having Cheez-Its and apple juice for snack later. Curt steps into a storage room. Trish steps out of the napping room and with an understanding smile on her face, gives Patti a little hug.

While they are waiting for Curt, Patti and her mother are standing on a large rug that is surrounded by shelves containing play dough, blocks, assorted toys, games, puzzles, pencils, markers, crayons, and various kinds of paper. The children have access to all of these materials during play, but they remain on the shelves unless they are retrieved by the children. Curt and Trish feel that if they set out materials, they may put a limit on the choices the children will make. Harry and Colin have pulled out a set of wooden blocks and are building what looks like a road. Patti almost smiles when Harry makes a silly face at her.

Two steps lead down from the main part of the classroom to a smaller nook which houses an easel, a large shelf containing art materials, and two tables with small chairs. When the rest of the classroom is busy, this area serves as a quiet place for working and playing. Some of the children are sitting in this area, talking and working with markers and papers.

Curt steps out of the storage room with a large pillow and sets it under the climber. Finally, Patti is ready to be put down. She is still teary-eyed, but she plops herself onto the pillow, symbolically giving her mother permission to leave.

Now that you have begun to develop a sense of the physical, and perhaps the socioemotional, environment of Curt and Trish's classroom, we are ready to consider the kind of literacy exploration that occurs here. This classroom is the most peaceful I have ever seen. While I think this kind of atmosphere is desirable, it is not always easy to achieve. This chapter looks at elements that contribute to a successful learning environment—one in which teachers are knowledgeable about teaching and find it stimulating and challenging, children are actively sharing and exploring their worlds, and parents feel confident that their children not only receive an education, but are also respected, loved, and treated as important people.

Curt and Trish have provided a *print-rich play environment* for their children. The classroom is filled with a variety of reading and writing materials to be used for all kinds of purposes. When the children or teachers see a good reason to use print in their play, they have no trouble finding a way to do so. Our exploration of literacy through play in this classroom starts by looking at how Curt and the children plan for play.

Planning for Play

Mike draws several little pictures on a piece of paper and then writes some letters. He brings the paper to Curt.

Mike: Look at my plan.

Curt: Read it to me.

Mike: Sea Quest.

Curt: Sea Quest.

Mike: Blocks . . . Kung Fuey . . .

When Mike finishes, Curt jots a few notes to himself so that he will remember what Mike has told him. Meanwhile, Harry has placed a fresh piece of paper over his finished plan. He is tracing what he has drawn and written. Mike notices.

Mike: Did you mess up?

Harry: I didn't mess up, Mike, I'm just doing copies of it. Guess what I'm doing, Curt. I'm making copies of my plan.

Curt: Oh, so right underneath it is the other copy, and you're tracing it?

Harry: Yeah, exactly.

The children in Curt and Trish's classroom often begin their play periods by writing, drawing, telling, or pantomiming a *plan* for play. *Plans* are responses to a question such as "What would you like to do today?" or "What are you going to play?" Often, while the older children write or draw their plans, the younger children tell them, or act them out. The children are not required to follow their plans, but they often do. Planning is a worthwhile pursuit in Curt and Trish's classroom for several reasons:

- It helps children find a focus for play.
- Teachers get information for setting up the play environment.
- Teachers find ideas for getting play back on track.
- Children use oral language to explain and inform.
- It provides a meaningful context for literacy exploration.

Children Find a Focus

First, planning helps the children to deliberately find a focus for play. With a plan in mind, the children move directly into an activity rather than wander the classroom looking for something to do. If a child has difficulty entering into social play situations, Curt can use the plans to locate others who have mutual interests for the day and help these children begin their play together. If others do not have similar interests, Curt may play with the child initially and perhaps work toward drawing others into the event. Over time, planning facilitates children's independence as players because it requires them to make decisions, experience the consequences of these decisions, consider alternatives, and verbally share their thoughts and ideas—all important play skills.

Teachers Get Information for Setting Up the Environment

Play plans also help Curt to set up the play environment in a constructive way. In the vignette, we saw that Mike and Harry were interested in playing Kung Fu. Knowing this, Curt was able to support their play by asking about the materials they would need and by making sure that they would have enough space to carry out the play. As the children in the classroom share their plans, Curt talks with many of them about the materials they will need. Often, he goes to the storage room and brings out special materials, or he helps children find the things they need on the shelves in the classroom. Conflicts that arise during play often stem from children not having the materials they need, not having enough space to play, not having access to materials, or having to use materials that are in disrepair (Johnson, Christie, and Yawkey 1987). Curt's planning with the children helps him determine whether the materials and space for play are sufficient.

In reading the vignette, you may have noticed that Curt takes *anecdotal notes* at planning time. Anecdotal notes are brief records of classroom events that a teacher considers worth remembering. As the children are planning, Curt jots down notes about their play interests. Over time, he can look for emerging patterns in their play and can use this information to collect materials that will contribute to an interesting and meaningful play environment.

Teachers Find Ideas for Getting Play Back on Track

A third way in which plans are useful is that they help Curt to keep play on a productive track. We *manage* play in order to meet the multiple safety, health, social, emotional, and cognitive needs of all of the children in a classroom. A well-managed play environment promotes growth in all of these areas. When Curt feels that one of these areas is at stake, he can use the plans to sensitively help the "culprits" change the course of their play. Mike and Harry's Kung Fu play started out in a constructive mode, with their stacking and organizing blocks, but soon they began to kick, chop, and whoop. Their play had become boisterous and noisy. Curt reminded them that some of the children in the school were sleeping. Apparently, however, Kung Fu players need to make noise and knock things over. "That's how we do Kung Fu," Mike explained. "They do karate things," Harry added. They tried to play with quiet vocalizations and with gentle chops and kicks, but the play began to lose its vitality. When it looked like things might get out of hand again, Curt referred back to the children's plans:

Curt: Are you still planning to play Sea Quest?

Mike: Yeah.

Curt: Do you need some sea animals? I could find a basket of sea animals.

Mike: Yeah, that's what we need to play Sea Quest.

Curt: Okay.

The plans helped Curt to gently guide the children toward a more appropriate form of indoor play. It is important to note, however, that Curt did not attempt to redirect the play at first. In developmentally appropriate classrooms, working with children in disruptive play situations is an important part of the overall teaching that occurs. Curt attempted to work with the children within the context of the Kung Fu play, and only when that faltered did he suggest another play option. Thus, the children's status as real people with feelings and good ideas was maintained.

Children Use Oral Language

A fourth reason that planning is a worthwhile endeavor in Curt and Trish's classroom is that it provides children with an opportunity to use oral language to explain and inform. Because of the nature of preschool writing and drawing, children often must tell about their creations so that others will know what they are intended to communicate. The written (or drawn) plans serve as a scaffold for the oral communication because children use them to guide the direction of their talk. As they explain what they have drawn or written, they systematically point out each item, using the pictures or letters as a resource for expressing each idea. What a precursor to reading conventional text! When the children present their plans orally or through pantomime, the objects around the classroom provide the scaffold. The children look systematically around the room as they think about, act out, or tell what they are going to do. It is important that children become competent at explaining and informing, or at putting an idea "into words in such a way that their listener(s) and/or reader(s) will understand it . . ." (Lindfors 1991, 364). Developing a clear message for an audience is fundamental to effective communication.

The written plans and play objects around the room are not the only scaffold for learning to effectively communicate. Curt, too, provides a scaffold as the children explain their plans. He supports the children's talk as he asks questions ("Where's the Kung Fu part on your plan?"), clarifies things for himself ("These are the two bricks and the piece of foam?"), and expands on what the children are saying ("Oh, so right underneath it is the other copy and you're *tracing* it"). *Scaffolding questions* both respond to and elaborate on children's ideas; they help children to smoothly "grow into the intellectual life of those around them" (Vygotsky 1978, 88). Opportunities to scaffold children's talk arise each time a plan is presented.

A Meaningful Context for Literacy Exploration

Tia has written several random strings of letters.

Curt: Tia, what do you have on your plan?

Tia: [*pointing to a string of letters*] I'm going to color with Karla and then I'm going to color a picture.

Curt: So, are you writing all that down?

Tia: Yes.

Curt: [*pointing to a different string of letters*] Tell me what you're writing here . . .

The final reason planning is worthwhile is that it is a meaningful context for literacy exploration. Curt doesn't ask the children to plan because he wants to teach them to read and write; he asks them to plan because he believes it enhances their play. However, he recognizes that the plans are a good medium for facilitating literacy. In developmentally appropriate classrooms, children are taught within the contexts of actual living conditions (Dewey 1938). Skills and strategies for reading and writing are taught, as they are needed, to individual learners (Weaver 1994). Plans serve a real-life function for Curt and the children, and they also provide a good opportunity to teach.

Literacy Through Play

After the children plan for play, they move on to engage in their chosen activities. During play, the physical environment, the rich episodes of pretend, and the complex interactions that take place all contribute to the children's construction of knowledge.

The Literacy-Oriented Play Environment

Karla is playing as a physician. She has a stethoscope around her neck and some other tools from a doctor's kit beside her. Trish is playing as a mother who brings her two young children in for a checkup. Karla takes notes on a clipboard as she interviews Trish:

Karla: How old is your baby?

Trish: Well, one is six months old and the other is twenty months old.

Karla: Does she eat any food?

Trish: Well, the one that is six months old, he eats a lot of sweet potatoes.

Karla: What's the other one's favorites?

Trish: She eats a lot of cheese crisps.

Karla: What else?

Trish: Yogurt.

Karla: Well, what else does she like?

Trish: Spaghetti, but not the baby.

Karla: Ku-betti. Ku-betti. [*said while writing*]

Karla: The reason I got another [appointment] for today is the baby has a period.

Trish: What's a period?

Karla: When blood comes out.

Play is a wonderful medium for investigating the world. As children play, they explore their own place in the world as well as the perspectives, actions, and routines of the members of their sociocultural communities (Kantor, Miller, and Fernie 1992). As Karla plays, she is exploring the world of a physician and probably, too, of a mother. She asks Trish the kinds of questions that physicians typically ask. She wants to know the ages of the children and what they eat. She provides a diagnosis for the baby and then answers further questions. Karla even leaves the area to consult with Tia (another physician) about the diagnosis.

Each time Karla asks a question of Trish, she writes down the response. Although she is not writing conventionally, she is exploring a function of written language (taking notes to remember and reflect) and is gaining good practice with forming letters, breaking words into syllables (Ku-betti), and taking notes. Karla's physician-like note taking is one little step down her road to literacy. Each time she uses written language in play, she is taking another step. "Having once had an encounter [with written language], subsequent encounters are governed at least in part by their understanding of what worked last time" (Harste, Burke, and Woodward 1981, 13). In other words, children use language to fine-tune language. Every encounter matters.

Karla's literacy exploration would not be possible without accessible literacy materials. In this case, she has a clipboard, a pen, and a pad of paper. If we want children to explore literacy through play, then it makes sense to ensure that their play areas are filled with as many literacy materials as possible. Stocking all of the play areas with paper and pencils is a good start. These materials are flexible and can be used for many purposes. Play areas that are tied to specific themes can be equipped with literacy materials related to those themes. For example, a physician's office could contain an eye chart, a yardstick, a scale, magazines, posters, a reference manual, and a scheduling book.

A restaurant could contain menus, pencils, order pads, chalk, and chalkboards. (See Chapter 6 for further discussion of setting up the literate environment.) Curt and Trish's play environments help these children learn about written language as they play.

Developing Literacy Through Play

Harry and Aster are playing as waiters. Curt orders crab.

Harry: I wonder how you really spell *crab.*

Aster: How *do* you?

Harry: Um, I can't really remember.

Aster: But, you could sound it out.

Harry utters several of the sounds in the word crab while writing the letters K-R-R-B-A. Aster repeat the sounds, and also writes the letters.

Harry: Cra-buh . . . uh. And maybe an *O* at the end. Do you think so?

Aster: Yeah.

Harry: All right. [*Writes* O.] Curt, does that spell *crab?*

Curt: I read it as *crab.* Do you read it as *crab?*

Harry: I don't know.

Curt: What do you think it says?

Harry: Uh, *crab.*

Curt: Yes.

Harry: Ooh! Cool. *Crab's* so easy. I didn't know we could write that!

Curt: You sounded it out.

Harry: Yeah!

Aster: K-R-R-B-A-O.

Harry: Oh! We wrote *crab.* Now we know how to write *crab.* I didn't know we could really write.

Curt orders cake (K-A-K) and milk (M-O-K) next. Aster writes the order (see Figure 2–1).

Children become literate as they explore the *functions* and *features* of written language. A *function* is a reason, or a purpose, for using print. Exploration of function is a natural part of play because children need written language to support their play themes. They label things, record medical information, write in appointment books, read menus, use telephone books, order food, and take down restaurant orders. Play provides a natural and meaningful context for exploring the many functions of written language. A *feature* is a

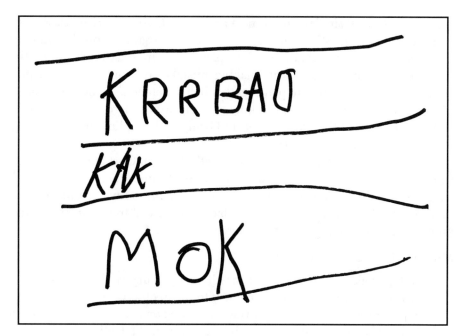

Figure 2–1. Aster's Restaurant Order

letter-sound relationship, a grammatical structure, or anything that has to do with the meaning of written language. Any time children write, read, or talk about sounds, spellings, or the meaning of words, they are exploring the features of written language. You can see how an exploration of function leads to an exploration of features. Once children have a reason to use print, they naturally explore its features.

What functions and features of written language are Aster and Harry exploring in the vignette? The list serves a particular function. In this case, when they take it into the kitchen to prepare Curt's food, it helps them to remember, and to show others, what Curt has ordered. As they write down Curt's order (crab, cake, and milk), they discuss the formation of letters and talk about and try out a number of sounds. They also choose a list as their format, which makes good sense, because waiters need to be quick!

As Harry, Aster, and the other children in Curt and Trish's classroom play together, they often scaffold one another toward new understandings. Children who play together in a literate environment are frequently seen "putting together the 'pieces' of their individual mental work, [and] building up their knowledge in the discourse process" (Pontecorvo and Zuccchermaglio 1990, 70). For example, Harry worked arduously to come up with the sounds in the word *crab* as Aster prompted, made suggestions, and supported his approximations. Visit play time almost any day in Curt and Trish's classroom, and you will hear questions such as "What does that say?" "How do you write that?" and "What does that mean?" In play, there are relatively few negative consequences for sharing ideas, making mistakes or not doing something "right." Allowing children to play together helps them to take the risks that are involved in thinking aloud. A thinking, sharing atmosphere makes it easy for children to sort out their knowledge and bring their implicit understandings to a conscious level (Barnes 1993).

Through the play, talk, and shared reflections in Curt and Trish's classroom, the children encounter numerous opportunities to construct knowledge about written language. Often, an adult becomes involved in this process. When this happens, the adult can facilitate the children's construction of knowledge by modeling aspects of literacy.

Modeling Literacy Through Play

> Todd, Angie, and Karla are in the climber playing as king-, queen-, and princess-monster. Curt is sitting next to them, observing. He takes a piece of paper from a nearby shelf, writes something on it, and folds it in half. He picks up a box and turns to the children, saying, "Pretend this is a mailbox and I have a letter for the king and queen and the princess."

Curt is *modeling* a use of written language. Literacy modeling in play involves using written language within the context of the play—as a participant. The goal is to encourage children to incorporate written language into their play or to help them elaborate on a literacy event that is already taking place. This type of contribution requires that the teacher carefully interpret the children's play focus. If the contribution is not based on cues from the children, they may simply not pay attention to it, or worse, they may lose the control of the play to the adult (Schrader 1991). As *interpreters* of children's play, teachers become aware of their play focus before entering the play (Monighan-Nourot et al. 1987).

None of the children in the vignette are conventional readers, yet Curt gives them a note written in an adult hand, modeling conventional writing. The children do not hesitate to read it.

Angie: [*to Karla*] Can you read this?

Karla: Yes. It says, "To king-monster and queen-monster and the princess-monster, queen of all. And prince. I would like to invite you to dinner at The-All-Meat-Eaters, at once, tonight."

Although the reading does not match what Curt has actually written, he is delighted to see that the children are exploring some important features and functions of written language. Through their talk they explore the kinds of information and language typically included in an invitation. Knowing what to expect will make future invitations easier to interpret and read. They are also exploring the function of an invitation as they take Curt up on his offer, and join him later for dinner. Curt accepts the children's interpretation of the writing, satisfied that they have engaged in the process of assigning predictable meaning to print and that they have explored a useful function of written language.

The next modeling event leads to a teachable moment. As you read the two vignettes in the next section, see if you can identify when the teachable moment occurs.

Capturing Teachable Moments

Aster and Curt are seated at a table, wearing mail hats. A mailbox is set up nearby. "I'm writing a letter," Curt says, as he fills out an envelope. Aster responds, "I think it's for me because my name's on it." Aster tells Curt that she, too is writing letters: one for Curt and one for Mike. Curt puts his letter in the envelope, puts a stamp on it, and tells Aster, "I'm going to mail it."

Let's think about Curt's modeling. He has placed a letter in an envelope, put names on it, stamped it, and is now preparing to mail it. His focus is on modeling a function of written language (Aster can only get this letter if her name is on it). As he writes, he naturally models some specific features (the placement of the names and the writing on the envelopes). When you model in your classroom, keep in mind that you are modeling both functions and features every time you write or read. Depending on the needs of the child and the context of the play situation, you can choose your focus. As they continue their play, Curt finds an opportune moment to teach Aster something new:

Aster places her two letters into two envelopes and they both go to the mailbox. Curt notices that she has not written any names on her envelopes.

Curt: Aster, how am I going to tell which one's mine?

Aster: Mike's has a three on it. Yours has a two on it. [*holding up one of the identical envelopes*] That's yours.

Curt: You mean [you wrote that] on the inside?

Aster: Yeah.

Curt: How—if you weren't here—how could I have known it was mine? Any ideas? . . .

A *teachable moment* occurs when a child is on the verge of making an important new discovery and the context is "just right" for making it. When Curt and Aster go to the mailbox and he notices that she has not addressed her letters, this is the teachable moment. Curt is always watching for these moments as he plays and interacts with children.

Teachable moment strategies involve knowledgeably observing children and seeking out relevant opportunities to help them extend their understandings. You probably do this without noticing it. When the context seems just right, you help a child try out a new idea or see something in a new way, following the child's lead. Your help is based on what you have learned about the child, and based on what you know about development. When you are successful at capturing teachable moments, you value children's contributions to their learning, and at the same time provide relevant input from the adult perspective.

Substantive Responses

Teachable-moment teaching may seem like something we just do naturally. When a child shows you a piece of writing, or art, it is very easy to automatically say, "Good job!" "That was a neat idea!" or "I like that!" On the other hand, if you want to use this moment to teach, you make a substantive response. If you only have a moment, you might say, "You drew a lot of dots on that page" or "When you put all of that together, you made an enormous collage" or "I see that you put some periods with what you wrote." If you have more time, you might say, "Read this part to me." "How did you come up with the idea?" "Where did you learn how to do this?"

A substantive response does at least as much, if not much more, as simply saying "good job." Substantive responses show children that you are aware of their developing competency, as do comments like "good job," but they also teach something. Substantive responses acquaint children with descriptive terms that are used by adults; they help children reflect back on the work they have done; they do not emphasize the product over the process. This is important because young children often attach more significance to the process (the act of developing the piece), than they do to the end product. Also, substantive responses are more sincere because they are tailored to what the child has actually accomplished. A substantive response is made with the intention of extending an event, encouraging a child's use of language to share ideas, or helping a child to think about something in a new way.

After Play

Angie: I played with Karla on the climbing structure and pretended it was a haunted house . . .

Diego: I played with the car and the climbing structure and I was werewolf and animals . . .

Karla: I took a nap and I drawed, and Tia woked me up three times . . .

At the end of play periods, Curt often asks the children to tell, to act out, to sculpt, or to write about what they have done that day. Reflecting on play in this way provides yet another context for sharing language and listening to and telling stories. Curt helps the children with their sharing by saying, "Tell about something you did today that you really liked" or "Todd, you were doing something by yourself. What were you doing?" Sometimes he sets a timer because the children love to talk. Curt, I'm sure, would be glad to listen, but the other listeners get restless if this event takes more than a few minutes.

Curt takes a turn, too, modeling effective sharing, and making a point to be a model listener. He says, "Right now I am listening to Karla" or "Do you hear what Tia is telling us?" "We want children to be able to tell (or follow the telling of) a 'story,' a series of related events, either real or imagined, in an orderly time sequence. As adults, we use language in this way a great deal": to inform, persuade, and make sense of the world (Lindfors 1991, 356). The narration that children use to plan for and describe their play helps them to develop this competence.

Developmentally Sensitive Teaching

Curt supports children in different ways, based on what he knows about typical patterns of development and about individual children. At play time, his roles range from observer to co-player to follower to leader. He takes no downtime, but instead remains intent on the children's activity. Too often in preschool classrooms teachers use play time to catch up on their numerous classroom responsibilities. Lesson plans and notes to families are written, shelves are organized, an art project is prepared. In a developmentally appropriate classroom, play time is teaching time. Teachers "stimulate and support children's engagement in play and child-chosen activities . . . extend[ing] the child's thinking and learning . . . by posing problems, asking questions, making suggestions, adding complexity to tasks, and providing information, materials and assistance . . ." (Bredekamp and Copple 1997, 128). Curt is available to support play because he and Trish do a great deal of preparation before the children come to school, and then divide their responsibilities when the children are present. Their kind of teaching takes a tremendous effort, but it is definitely worth it.

A VISIT TO A FIRST GRADE

North Road Elementary School is situated on a busy street in Fenton, a small Michigan town. Christine Eaton is one of four first-grade teachers at the school. She has thirty students this year. She teaches only in the morning, sharing her classroom with Gwen, who teaches the children in the afternoon.

Over the past few years, Christine has diligently worked toward implementing developmentally appropriate practices in her classroom. As part of the requirements for a Master of Arts degree in Early Childhood Education, she conducted a study in which she investigated, among other things, the use of *centers* to facilitate literacy. A *center* is an area of the classroom in which a set of related materials is arranged for exploration, construction, or dramatic play. For example, a block center that is designed for literacy exploration might include a set of wooden blocks, a basket full of small vehicles, and writing materials for making road signs, store signs, or maps. Typical centers in early childhood classrooms include art, library/listening/writing, blocks, dramatic play, science/discovery, manipulatives/mathematics, music, and woodworking (Brewer 1992).

The Classroom at Center Time

Walking into Christine's classroom at center time, you might say, "This is a place for talking, thinking, and hands-on learning!" The children's desks are arranged in groups of four in the interior part of the classroom. Centers are arranged around the perimeter of the classroom, but extend onto the floor between the desks. Some children have carried center materials to their desks so that they have extra space to work. About ten of the desks are occupied by children who are writing, doing puzzles, playing with math manipulatives, and reading. About fifteen children are working in the centers around the perimeter of the classroom. They are painting, reading from a big book, writing things on clipboards, and reporting news from the weather center. All of the children are talking, talking, talking! "Those crayons are brand new." "What does *brand* mean?" . . . "I wrote my eight in cursive." "No, there's not a cursive eight. You don't do numbers in cursive." . . . "Know why my eyes are green? Because my last name is *Green*." . . . "This is Seth Blacksmith with a little draft news. We're getting a few precipitation with sunny and hot. We might get a little rainy." Christine is sitting at a low table toward the back of the classroom reading a story with a small group of children. Most of the twenty-five children who are working at the centers seem to be engaged in productive activity. They are talking, writing, reading, and solving many problems without the help of their teacher. How does Christine make this happen? Let's start by looking at the centers she arranges.

Christine sets up sixteen centers each week. The most common are arranged in the following ways:

- *Dramatic Play.* A hinged-plywood stage is turned into a variety of dramatic play settings, including a post office, a pet store, a grocery store, a travel agency, and a puppet theater. (This center will be our focus.)

- *Browsing Box.* A rocking chair on a carpeted area serves as a place for individual reading or partner reading. Nearby bookshelves contain a browsing box with a variety of children's literature as well as books that the children have created.
- *Listening Center.* A small shelf containing books, tapes, headphones, and tape recorders serves as a listening center.
- *Big Books.* An easel with a Big Book and a pointer serves as a place for shared reading. The books that Christine sets out are usually related to the content-area theme that the class is pursuing. For example, when the class was studying water and the water cycle, Christine set out a variety of books that had something to do with water.
- *Science.* A science table is set up for a variety of kinds of discovery. For example, a sink/float table was set up when the children were studying water and the water cycle.
- *Manipulatives/Math.* Manipulatives, puzzles, and board games are stacked on a shelf, but are brought out by the children to function as a center. They usually bring these materials to their desks or use them on the floor.
- *Art.* An art table is stocked with materials for making a variety of projects. The projects typically tie in with content area pursuits. For example, the children created underwater creatures when they were studying water and the water cycle.
- *Writing.* A writing center includes paper, crayons, and pencils. Christine often assigns a general topic for this area: "Write a story that has something to do with water" or "Today you can write a letter to a friend."
- *Word Collecting.* A clipboard and pen are used to "read and write the room." Children walk around the classroom recording interesting pieces of written language.
- *Painting.* An easel is set up with paint and large paper.
- *Computer.* A computer is set up with a variety of games.
- *Pocket Chart.* A large pocket chart serves a variety of purposes. For example, sentence strips from a short story are set out for the children to place in sequential order.

Every Monday, Christine explains any new centers and tells how many of the children she thinks will fit into them at once. At this time, she designates some centers as "have-tos." Have-to centers must be visited because they are directly tied to specific curricular goals. For example, part of Christine's science program involves an exploration of the properties of sinking and floating objects. If the science center is set up with two bins of water and an array of objects to test, and the class is going to read about and discuss the properties of sinking and floating objects, then this becomes a have-to center. As Christine designs the centers, she keeps in mind the content-area concepts her children are expected to develop. Typically, the themes of many of the centers are connected to one another by a social studies or science-related theme the class is pursuing.

Because it is important to Christine that her children explore key content-area concepts in as many different ways as possible, she often recasts the curriculum through play (Van Hoorn et al. 1993). In other words, she sets up the play centers in such a way that her children can use them to explore content-area concepts. For example, while studying letter writing, the children played in a post office; while studying water, the children played with sinking and floating objects; while studying homes, the children played in a construction center.

Preparing Children for Using Play Centers

If, like Christine, you like to spend some of your center time working with small groups of children, then the organizational techniques you use look quite different from those used by Curt. Actually, in a preschool classroom, it is not advisable to let children play without support. The preschool curriculum is centered around play, which means that the teaching must also be centered around play. Also, preschoolers need much social support during play because they are still learning to express themselves, to share, to listen to others, and to play cooperatively. If you teach kindergarten, you may be able to pull yourself away from the children's play for short periods of time. Christine feels that it would be ideal to spend all of center time at the centers (and sometimes she does), but she also finds that this is an ideal time to work with small groups.

Although finding a system that "works" will vary from teacher to teacher and from year to year, it might be helpful to think about the following techniques as you prepare children to use play centers: creating a manageable plan for the children to work through the centers, demonstrating or modeling possible uses of materials, providing time for exploration of materials, and modeling scripts for interacting.

Planning

At center time, the children are divided into four groups. Following techniques suggested by Fountas and Pinnell (1996), Christine uses a large chart containing icons of the sixteen centers to show each group four centers from which they may choose. Young children need a visual display of the centers that are available to help them organize their thinking and make their selections. The chart is arranged in four columns. Christine just needs to rotate each group's names along the top of the columns to let them know their four options. Once the names are rotated, the children fill out their plans by circling their four options and writing down which of the four they will actually use.

Most children complete their plans within three to four minutes. Because plans are finished one by one the transition from seats to centers runs smoothly. As plans are completed, Christine checks them to make sure that the children have selected the correct four options. If a have-to center has been forgotten on the plan, she lets the child know. When center time is over, the children revisit their plans, writing down what they have accomplished. It is important that children who work independent of their teacher learn to set goals for themselves and to complete center activities (Morrow 1997). Planning provides a window of time for children to think about their options and to select those that seem interesting and achievable within the forty-five-minute center time. Revisiting plans helps the children to reflect on whether they have accomplished their goals.

Modeling Possible Uses of Materials

As we saw in Curt and Trish's classroom, some teachers observe children's play before modeling. Because Christine works with small groups during center time she often models possible uses of the materials in a center before opening it to the children. The following vignette illustrates how she introduced a new store center. The store carried a variety of small objects either in packs of ten or in ones. The children were to fill out an order form with their selections and present it to the clerk.

Christine: I'm going to demonstrate this with a friend. Anne, would you come up here? Today this is going to be a store. [*Christine fills out an order form, showing the children what she is doing.*] I'm going to look at Anne and say, "Excuse me. I would like to buy . . . fifty-four crayons."

Christine hands her order form to Anne, and Anne begins to count the crayons one by one, instead of by tens.

Christine: Can you think of an easier way? Can you think of a different way to do this? [*pointing to the packs of ten*] These are tens.

Jason: She can count five tens.

Anne counts five tens and four ones and gives the crayons to Christine.

Christine: I'm going to say, "Thanks, Anne," and I'm going to check to make sure I have the right amount.

Christine's recasting of the mathematics curriculum into play is quite evident here. The children can be as creative as they like while playing in the center, but one thing Christine hopes they will do is to practice counting by ten. As she models the use of materials in this center, she is sure to address this issue. The demonstration has given the children an overview of the materials in the center and they have ideas for how they might use them.

Providing Time for Exploration

A toy cash register and cashier stand are part of the store center, but Christine does not mention these in her demonstration. These props are familiar to the children and have been a regular part of many play centers. If these props had been new to the classroom, Christine may have given the children time to explore them before including them in a play center. "Familiarity with the setting and its objects frees children to go beyond physically exploring them to using them as springboards for episodes of pretend play" (Roskos 1995, 8–9). Putting the materials on a shelf or a table for a week or two before including them in a play center is a good way to give the children a chance to explore them. Another option is to simply expect that the children will take some time to explore the materials before moving into sociodrama. Christine's children typically spend only one or two days in a center, so in this classroom, it is important that they can move right into sociodrama and not spend all of their time in the center exploring.

Modeling Scripts

As Christine models the use of the store center, she is also modeling the scripts typically used between customers and clerks in a store: "I'm going to look at Anne and say, 'Excuse me, I would like to buy . . . ,'" "Anne, can you get me fifty-four crayons . . . ," "I'm going to check to make sure I have the right amount . . . ," "Thank you, Anne . . ." A *script* is a generally accepted way of interacting in a given social situation. Christine doesn't expect her children to do or say exactly what she does and says, but her language and actions are good models for children who may not have experience with shopping. Some children do not shop with their families, and do not know what to do or expect in a store. Christine's demonstration helps the children come into the play with similar expectations and a basic idea for what they might do.

A lack of familiarity with a play center's theme may put a limit on what children will do. When Christine and Gwen had a travel agency set up in their room, Gwen reflected that the children seemed unable to relate to the theme. She reflected that the notion of traveling to other states seemed "too far from home." Indeed, when I observed the center, I noticed that the play started off nicely, but soon lost its appeal:

Callie: You be the customer. What would you like? Because we have that.

Jason: [*filling out a ticket*] How do you spell *Florida?*

Callie: [*goes through ticket stubs and finds one with* Florida *written on it*] F-L-O-R-I-D-A. [*Jason gives the ticket to Callie, who fills in the arrival and departure times.*] And here's your Florida ticket. Your check is fifty-five. Hold on—[*pushes buttons on cash register*] your total is, sir, twenty-nine cents and fifty-nine dollars.

So far, so good. As the children play out the roles of travel agent and traveler, they explore the functions of a cash register, a check, and a ticket. They also explore a feature of written language as they work collaboratively to solve a spelling question.

Jason moves to the inside of the agency, telling Callie that he wants to be the agent now.

Callie: Jason, you got to be my customer!

Jason: I did!

Callie: You got to do it again. You're not a very nice customer. You got to let me work until I have a day off.

Callie is not ready to move away from the role of travel agent, but Jason no longer wants to be the customer. It seems as if he considers his play complete because he has purchased one ticket. It is possible that his prior knowledge about travel agencies is not enough to help him carry his play forward. If he had more experience with travel agencies, he may have attempted to plan another trip, to ask questions about Florida, to get tickets for family members, or to pull up some chairs to construct an airplane. Lack of familiarity with a theme is always a risk when we choose play themes for children. Perhaps Gwen was right when she reflected that the children were having a difficult time connecting with the theme. If we expect the children to play creatively and to go beyond what our modeling and demonstrations suggest, then the theme must be familiar. (Familiarity is an issue that is discussed further in Chapter 5.)

Dramatic Retelling

Nicholas: Little Pig, Little Pig, let me in!

Tony: Not by the hair of my chinny-chin-chin. We just built our hard house of bricks.

Dramatic retelling is the act of retelling a story or a part of a story using masks, costumes, puppets, props, pantomime, or language and gesture. A book, script, or other piece of literature (such as a story written by a child) may or may not be used to support the retelling as it is taking place. The children in Christine's classroom can often be seen with masks on their faces, animatedly retelling a favorite fairy tale, with puppets on their hands, giggling their way through a story the class has read together, or with pencils in hands, writing and/or creatively illustrating retellings.

Dramatic retelling is more than fun—it facilitates learning. When children participate in dramatic retelling, they transform their understandings from one sign system (oral language) to another (dramatic movement, written language, gestures, pantomime). To do so, they must reorganize, rethink, and repackage their ideas about what they have read. In the example above, Tony transforms what he has read just a little by adding, "We just built our hard house of bricks." Tony is really thinking. He is making it clear to the audience why a brick house makes sense, and why, as the Third Little Pig, he is so safe. Children gain new perspectives by transforming what they know from one sign system to another (Short, Harste, and Burke 1996).

Teaching Children to Retell

Although Christine encourages her children to dramatically retell stories without her help, she sometimes walks the children through the process. Children need experience and guided practice in order to learn to retell effectively (Morrow 1997). Guided practice helps children to include important story elements, and to retell the story in a logical sequence. Christine uses whole-class instruction to teach dramatic retelling. First, she makes sure the whole class has had a chance to either read or listen to the story. It is a good idea to tell children before reading if they will be retelling a story because they listen differently (Morrow 1997). Listening to a story more than once may be also helpful, as it has been found to lead to richer retellings that are characterized by an integration of children's world knowledge with the words and ideas of the author (IRA/NAEYC 1998). Once the children have heard the story (at least once), Christine helps them organize their thinking with some questions. First, she asks about the *characters:* Who are the characters? Who do we need first? Who comes next? Who comes last? This is just what she wants them to do as they play by themselves.

After talking with the class about characters, Christine asks for volunteers to play the parts. As the volunteers take their positions, she and the children talk about the *setting.* This helps them move into a dramatic mode, because they must symbolically create props and figure out how to position themselves so that the setting becomes clear. The following vignette is part of a whole-class dialogue between Christine and her students:

The volunteers come up to the front of the room and take their positions. Christine addresses the remaining children:

Christine: Dana, tell me what happens first.

Dana: Do I have to read the story?

Christine: No, just tell us.

When Dana tells what happened first, the volunteers begin to act.

Christine: Tessa, what happens next . . . It's on the next page there. We've got to give Gregory his cue. What happens next?

Jason: He says that Sara ain't his friend.

Christine: Yes. Who knows what happens next?

As the story is told, Christine talks with the children about its *problem* and *resolution,* prompting them with questions such as Why did this happen to the character? How does he feel? What did he do? By going through the dramatic retelling process with the whole class, Christine provides the children with a framework to use when they work on their own with puppets, masks, or other props. The knowledge that stories are made up of certain parts makes them easier to interpret and dramatize. To reenact a story, children must consider its sequence (Christine uses the term *order*), setting, characters, problem, and resolution. This kind of exercise shows the children how to think about these story elements as they dramatically retell a story.

Writing or drawing a story before retelling it may also be a useful way of thinking about its parts and sequence. Christine sometimes invites her children to engage in written and drawn retellings at the writing table during center time. Figure 2–2 shows Leslie's drawn retelling of the story of *The Three Little Pigs.*

Figure 2–2. Leslie's Drawn Retelling of *The Three Little Pigs*

Meeting Individual Needs

Molly (Narrator): Introducing *The Three Little Pigs.* The first little pig said, "May I have some straw?"

Kassie (Wolf): Shhh! The wolf is supposed to say that, silly. "May I have some straw to build my house with?"

Providing time for retelling in a supportive environment is a good way to address children's individual needs. Christine often reads the stories to be used for dramatic retelling with small groups of children. This ensures that all of the children have had a chance, at least once, to successfully read through the text. The children come to the dramatic retelling center with various understandings and competencies. In play, these differences don't matter. Each child can comfortably participate in dramatic retelling because of the relatively risk-free nature of this event. Children are not asked to memorize lines, and they are encouraged to be creative as they retell. Asking young children to memorize lines or participate in many rehearsals would be considered a developmentally inappropriate practice for a school setting because it serves no real educational purpose (Raines and Isbell 1994). We can find better ways for children to spend their time. In dramatic retelling, there are few negative consequences for veering from the story line or not knowing what to say next.

We can't underestimate the support that children provide one another as they engage in dramatic retelling. If, like Christine, you are otherwise occupied while your children are playing, be assured that the natural scaffolding that occurs among children provides help for those who need it. The children in Christine's classroom are typically eager to support their friends when it helps them to get through the story. They provide cues for lines, they come out of character and tell others what to do next, and they read from the storybooks so that others have many cues to support their dramatization. Their facilitation of retelling knowledge for one another is just as important as the instruction Christine provides.

As children engage in dramatic retelling, they construct knowledge on a personal level as they transform the story ideas from one sign system to another, and they construct on a social level as they scaffold one another's understandings. Christine facilitates their construction of knowledge by providing props for retelling, by teaching children to retell, and by giving them many opportunities for practice.

Dramatic Play

In Curt and Trish's preschool classroom, we saw that becoming literate involves exploring the functions and features of written language, and that play provides many opportunities for this exploration. The same holds true in

kindergarten and first-grade classrooms, except that the functions ‹
and the feature exploration becomes more complex. We are going to
just one more vignette from Christine's classroom. As you read, think about
the functions and features of written language that the children are exploring:

Callie is standing behind the counter of the post office.

Callie: Did you write a letter to somebody, Kassie?

Kassie: Yeah. [*shows a series of squiggly lines*]

Callie: Just a bunch of lines?

Kassie: Yeah. [*attempts to give the letter to Callie*]

Callie: No. You got to weigh it.

Kassie: Oh, yeah. [*puts the letter on the scale*]

Callie: [*pushing the buttons on the cash register*] Fifteen cents and twenty-five.

*Adam comes to the post office and sits on the floor. He writes: CATSUARFUN
(cats are fun). He folds the letter and on the outside writes: To Cat. Adam. He
gives the letter to Nora, who is playing as a cat.*

Think about all the functions these children are exploring. They are weighing
with a scale, using a cash register, writing letters, exchanging pretend money,
and writing friendly notes. Think about all the features they are exploring.
They are inventing spellings, using punctuation, reading numbers, and creating written messages. Now think about the play environment in your own
classroom. If your children are exploring a variety of functions of written language, pat yourself on the back. If they also have the materials and the support
they need to explore a variety of features, give yourself a hug. You are well on
your way to helping your children become literate individuals who see reading and writing as enjoyable, useful, and well worth discovering.

Play may feel like a risky thing because you want to make sure that your children are spending their time as productively as possible. Not to fear! We have
seen children explore a variety of functions and features of written language,
and interpret and respond to literature in different ways—all through play.
Play allows teachers to respond to children's ideas, to help them elaborate on
their thinking, and to help them see the world of literacy through many lenses.
The key to successfully facilitating play is to know as much as possible about
the ways in which children think, learn, and develop knowledge, and then to
believe in their abilities to construct knowledge themselves.

3

Children Construct Knowledge About the World

It is nap time at preschool. Erin and Cindy are lying on their stomachs, face-to-face, writing in their journals and talking softly.

Erin: You know what? I'll never hear again, because when a person is deaf they don't never hear again . . .

Cindy: When I grow up I'm going to be blind, with my eyes not seeing.

Erin: Then you'll have to have a dog.

Cindy: Yeah, but I don't got working dogs. I got Clover and Millie and they're not working dogs.

Erin: You *can* work.

Cindy: Well, I don't think I'm going to have blind eyes . . .

Erin: I'll have to talk like something else. I can talk in sign language just like this. [*moving her hands, as if signing*]

Cindy: Or, I know. You can read with your hands from a piece of paper. From typing-dots. Little dots. [*moving her fingers, as if reading braille*]

How do children develop their unique ideas about the world? What are the forces that shape their ways of thinking? Somewhere, somehow, Erin and Cindy have learned about deafness, sign language, and the ability of the deaf to work; they have learned about blindness, braille, and the functions of working dogs; and they have developed language that is sophisticated enough to communicate these things. These children have obviously been out there in the world, watching, interacting, thinking, and inquiring. But just how has their learning occurred? What contributes to children's construction of knowledge? This chapter looks at the many forces that help children discover the world and sort out its myriad complexities.

The theories of Swiss scientist Jean Piaget and Russian psychologist Lev Vygotsky, two of the most prominent researchers ever to influence early childhood education, help us to understand that children's development is both pushed by inside forces and pulled by outside forces. As teachers, the more we understand these forces, the better able we are to provide instruction that is directly in tune with children's ways of thinking. So, let's dive in and explore how these forces work.

CONSTRUCTING KNOWLEDGE: INTERNAL AND SOCIAL WORLDS

Three-year-old Cory is standing in front of the shelves, looking at the new name tags on all of the children's cubbies. She steps in front of her own cubby, but looks hesitantly around the room, seeming unsure whether she has selected the right one. Her teacher, Leah, walks over to where Cory is standing. "Is that your cubby?" Cory looks puzzled as she points to the Y at the end of her name. "This has a J in it," she says. Leah responds, "That's not a J. That Y just has a curve in it."

Piaget and Vygotsky maintain that children's learning is influenced by *developmental* and *social* forces. When we say that learning is *developmental,* we mean that children construct their understandings about the world *for themselves.* As they go about their daily lives, they develop and test a never-ending series of little hypotheses, or ideas, about the ways in which the world works. As new experiences challenge their existing hypotheses, children refine them to accommodate the new information (Ferreiro and Teberosky 1982; Piaget 1952). When we say that learning is *social,* we recognize that children share language with others, try out their ideas in social situations, and receive feedback on their actions and hypotheses. Often, the feedback leads to changes in their earlier ways of thinking (Vygotsky 1978). So, learning is developmental and social at the same time. Children maintain a working model for what to expect from the world, and "[w]hen objects, events, and other people challenge the working model . . . the child is forced to adjust the model or alter the mental structures to account for the information" (Bredekamp and Copple 1997, 13).

In the vignette, Cory has a working model for how her name can look in print, but it is challenged when she sees the new name tag. It's time to adjust the model. Leah, her teacher, sees that the context is just right to help Cory make a new discovery and supplies some information that helps her to do so. As Cory works out this little puzzle she is *developing* her literacy knowledge, taking it a little step further than where it was before this experience. Her teacher's support and her own surprise at the name tag are the catalysts for change in her thinking. Learning involves a constant interplay of internal and social experiences. Social experiences influence and shape the ways in which children build their knowledge, and in turn, children's knowledge influences the input they will get from their social experiences (Bredekamp and Copple 1997; Dyson 1989; Goodman and Goodman 1990; Strickland and Strickland 1997).

Building Schema

To Piaget (1952), learning is a process of *schematic change,* or *schema building.* A *schema* can be thought of as a working model for understanding the world. We use our schemas to make sense of and to mentally organize all new events and experiences. Any time a new experience contributes a bit of information to the schema or makes the schema change, learning occurs. Schema building is not something that is unique to early childhood. It is something that we do throughout out lives, every time we encounter something new.

My ninety-four-year-old grandmother, Juanita Chenoweth, has never had a computer and definitely doesn't want one. "They're just too complicated." Until recently, she had never heard of electronic mail (e-mail). One day, my mother showed her a piece of e-mail that she had received just that morning. This presented a challenge to my grandmother's working model for mail. "How can this be?" she said. "What do you mean when you say that it 'came over the computer?'"

Assimilation and Accommodation

Because the concept of e-mail was new to my grandmother, she had to mentally organize the new information to make it sensible from her point of view. That's what learners do: they organize all new information to give it a comfortable place in their minds. They do this in one of two ways, through *assimilation* or *accommodation.* Perhaps my grandmother said to herself, "Aha! Yes, I knew this was coming. Here's one more way I can send and receive mail." If this were the case, it would be said that she had *assimilated* the new information into her existing schema for mail. *Assimilation* involves expanding an existing category of knowledge (a schematic category) to make room for new information. *Accommodation* occurs when new information does not fit so easily into the existing schema. Perhaps my grandmother said, "What? This doesn't make sense! This isn't like the kind of mail I know." When this happens, the new information must be *accommodated.* In accommodation, existing mental structures are significantly reorganized, or new structures are created. Perhaps my grandmother constructed a new little branch in her mail schema just for this outrageous thing called e-mail. Whether through assimilation or accommodation, she adapted the information to her schema.

Equilibrium

Adaptation to new experiences is referred to as *equilibrium*. Equilibrium is a necessary balancing mechanism between assimilation and accommodation. If individuals were to assimilate all new experiences, they would develop very broad schematic categories, and would have difficulty differentiating between things (my grandmother, for instance, would be unable to distinguish between all of the different kinds of mail that exist). If individuals were to accommodate all new experiences, they would develop very narrowly defined schemas, and would have difficulty connecting one thing to another (my grandmother would not see any similarities between my handwritten and my e-mail letters) (Hulit and Howard 1993). Assimilation and accommodation working together produce the *equilibrium* that allows the learner to efficiently organize and interpret new ideas.

As teachers, we want to know what leads to schema building so that we can set up the kind of environment and provide the kind of instruction that support this process. Schema building occurs as children engage in *action and exploration* (hands-on learning) and in *social collaboration.*

Action and Exploration

Erin and Clara have found some foam-backed hearts on a shelf in their classroom. They take them to a table and begin to squeeze and squish them and press them against their faces. They discover that the hearts can be crumpled into a fist, but they pop back into shape when released. The children decide to find some glue so that they can arrange their hearts on paper.

As they begin to work, Erin finds that the foam on the back of the hearts is absorbing all the glue. "Is this a problem, or what—this cotton stuff?" She adds enough glue to saturate the foam, and eventually, the heart sticks.

Meanwhile, Clara is having problems of her own. She is shaking her glue bottle and holding it upside-down, but no glue comes out. "Tell me how to do this," she urges. Erin instructs her friend to "stamp it down, squish it tight, keep squeezing!"

During the early childhood years, children spend many hours busily acting on and exploring their environments. They seem wired with the ability to learn. They touch, crumple, squeeze, squish, stamp, stretch, and stack. They push and pull things, bounce and bend them, roll and shake them, and they love mixing, categorizing, collecting, building, and taking things apart. What child has not reached a hand into a cupboard, rummaged through a purse, or built a tower of mashed potatoes? What child is not interested in pushing a doorbell, seeing how high blocks can be stacked, or cutting things with scissors? How many times have we had to tell parents, "Mona cut her hair"; "Shalonda packed play dough into her doll's head"; "John cut off his sleeve"; "Andrea cut her shoelaces"; "Oh, LaShaun's fingernails? Yes, well, it seems that one of my permanent markers got mixed in with the others . . ." Young children are notorious for closely inspecting and purposefully manipulating anything they can get their hands on. It is their way of learning about the world.

A Tool for Discovery

Piaget explains that children are curious about the world, and *acting on* it is how they come to understand it. As children act on objects—or experiment and play with them—they discover their properties and relationships. For example, by coloring and experimenting with pressure, children *discover* that pressing hard with a crayon yields a different result than pressing softly. Try to *tell* a child that and she just won't get it. By playing with balls in a variety of settings, children *discover* that rolling a round object on grass yields a different result than rolling it on pavement; rolling it with great force yields a different result than rolling it delicately. It is easy to build schemas about the properties of round objects by *playing* with round objects—much easier than by only being *told* about their properties.

Let's think about how assimilation and accommodation play a part in constructing knowledge through action and exploration. A child rolls a ball on pavement. It goes fast. She rolls a ball on a rug and notices that it goes fast, just as it did on pavement. She *assimilates* the information, saying to herself, "When balls are rolled, they go fast!" Then, the child rolls a ball on grass. "Oops!" she says, "Sometimes balls veer, curve, and roll slowly." Now she *accommodates,* having experienced a challenge to her working model for ball rolling. She creates a new little category in her schema—a place to keep information about rolling balls on bumpy surfaces. Accommodation and assimilation are always at work when children engage in hands-on exploration—provided they are working in a stimulating environment. For this reason, teachers in developmentally appropriate classrooms plan for children to engage in "a variety of concrete learning experiences . . . that promote their interest, engagement in learning, and conceptual development. Materials include, but are not limited to, blocks and other construction materials, books and other language arts materials, dramatic-play themes and props, art and modeling materials, sand and water with tools for measuring, and tools for simple science activities" (Bredekamp and Copple 1997, 126).

Piaget observed that when children are young, concrete objects are needed for exploration. Later, children are able to *distance* themselves from objects and perform mental manipulations (Hulit and Howard 1993). While a younger child needs the actual ball to reflect on its properties, an older child might hypothesize that a ball rolled on a rug would go faster than a ball rolled on grass. This explains why children in developmentally appropriate early childhood classrooms are seen playing, experimenting, acting on objects, and exploring, instead of listening to a teacher talk, watching her demonstrations, or filling out dittos and worksheets. Hands-on action and exploration are children's natural tools for discovering the world.

Acting on and Exploring Written Language

Expanding on Piaget's theories about action and exploration, Ferreiro and Teberosky (1982) refer to *written language* as an object of knowledge. When children begin to notice print, they engage in the same kinds of exploration as they engage in with all of the other objects in their worlds. On paper, they begin to experiment with lines, circles, loops, and squiggles, and eventually assign meaning to these forms. With books, they begin to explore "pretend reading" (Sulzby 1985), telling the stories not by reading the print, but by using picture clues and what they remember from previous readings. They begin, too, to assign meaning to the print they see in their environments, although these meanings may not be completely accurate. For example, a child may hypothesize that the writing on an ink pen says "pen" or that the writing on a Farmer Jack sign says "store." As their working models for written language are challenged, they will make accommodations in their thinking and eventually move toward conventional understandings.

As with any object of knowledge, children *act on* written language, discovering its properties and relationships. For example, by writing and inventing spellings, children discover the connections between letters and sounds. Emily, a first grader in Christine Eaton's classroom, was writing a letter one day and asked me how to spell *say*. "How do you think it's spelled?" I prompted. She answered, "*S-A*" and wrote down the letters, but then she paused and looked at me thoughtfully. "*Y!*" she said, "because it rhymes with *day*." I interpret this as an *assimilative* act. She has developed a little category in her schema for thinking about *-ay* words and *say* fits right in. By engaging in the act of writing, Emily is building a schema for spelling. I think that if I had told her how to spell the word, she would not have constructed any knowledge. She would have just taken the answer and moved on. Children learn not by adding on bits of knowledge to a knowledge base, but by "reconstructing the object, having comprehended its laws of composition" (Ferreiro and Teberosky 1982, 17).

When it comes to action and exploration, Piaget, Ferreiro, and Teberosky agree that exploring objects helps young children to discover the objects' properties and relationships. When children explore, they assimilate information, building on what they know, and make accommodations in their thinking when new ideas challenge their working models. For young children especially, hands-on exploration—which includes exploring print material and writing—is essential to constructing knowledge.

Peer Collaboration

While Piaget's research emphasizes children's self-construction of knowledge, he makes some interesting observations about social collaboration among peers. According to him, children start their lives as egocentric little beings who see the world from their own eyes and have a difficult time taking the perspective of others. When a two-year-old takes a toy from another two-year-old, neither considers the other's feelings or thoughts (DeVries and Kohlberg 1987). Taking the perspective of others is just not something that two-year-olds do. Piaget believes that interacting with peers is a way to overcome egocentricity, or, to *decenter* (Piaget and Inhelder 1969). When children decenter, they move from seeing the world in one way—their way—to coordinating a number of perspectives (DeVries and Kohlberg 1987). Instead of taking a toy without permission, a child becomes more likely to think, "I want that toy, but you'll cry if I take it." Over time, children's desire to play cooperatively helps them to accommodate others' ways of thinking. As they engage in play activity together, observe other children, and get feedback from them, they see that theirs is not the only way of thinking about and doing things.

Decentering has special significance when it comes to literacy development. For example, young children often write using scribble marks or random strings of letters. Becoming literate involves coming to know that written language has certain conditions that make it interpretable. Certain conventions are required if others are expected to read what we have written. Children often help one another come to this realization:

Sandra and Rodrigo are writing in their journals at preschool. Rodrigo has written a connected string of letterlike symbols:

Sandra: You're just playing. You're not doing anything . . . And you're scribbling, too, I hope you know.

Children are often prompted to change their working models for written language when other people present a challenge to their ways of thinking. They also change their models when the print itself presents a challenge. For example, the other day, my seven-year-old niece, Ivy, was reading through my pile of paper to recycle. She pointed out the word *they* on a page and asked,

"What does *T-H-E-Y* spell? Because, I know that *T-H-A-Y* spells *they.*" The text itself presented a challenge to Ivy's working model. Both people and print help children change their working models for written language in a move toward convention.

Piaget observed that as children play together they disagree on things, which can be a good thing because it induces a sense of cognitive conflict that drives new learning (Berk and Winsler 1995).

Harry and Mike are making play money, talking about where to put the commas in the numbers they are writing.

Mike: I'll do my own commas. I know how to do it. You go like this—[*writes a comma*]

Harry: After three.

Mike: [*pointing to his comma*] Right?

Harry: No, that goes in the wrong place.

Mike: Harry . . .

Harry: [*pointing to a different spot on Mike's paper*] *That's* the right place.

Mike: Harry, you're not in charge!

Harry: I know, but . . .

Mike: [*writes a comma where Harry has suggested*] This is in the right place, right?

Harry: [*looks at the paper*] Yeah, it is.

Mike: [*counts and writes another comma*] This is in the right place, right?

Harry: Yeah.

Mike continues to count and write commas. While, conventionally, he ought to be counting from right to left to place the commas, he is counting from left to right. For several of the numerals, his misunderstanding is inconsequential because they all contain six digits, but when he comes to a numeral with five digits, Harry notices the confusion and facilitates his friend's revision of his hypothesis:

Mike: Right place?

Harry: No, because *three.* After *three* you put a comma. [*Harry counts, pointing with his finger, from the right to the left, and writes a comma on Mike's money.*]

Mike: [*Mike checks Harry's work, but still counts in the wrong direction.*] No! That's after two.

Harry: But, it's after three right *here.* [*points to the right, showing the direction he is counting from; pauses*]

Mike: Oh! I was going like that [*moves his finger left to right to show the direction of his initial attempts at counting*]

When children play together, they often disagree on things, prompting them to articulate their viewpoints and take a second look at what they are doing or saying. When Harry and Mike's ideas clash, both children move forward. Mike learns the proper counting technique for placing commas, and Harry has the opportunity to verbally repackage his ideas in a way that makes sense to someone else.

Piaget believes that interactions between children are more powerful than interactions between children and adults, maintaining that when an adult is present children might simply view the adult as the expert and refrain from critically examining their own perspectives (Berk and Winsler 1995). In the vignette, Mike holds to his own way of counting commas until he accommodates to Harry's way of thinking. He says, "I'll do my own . . . You're not in charge . . . No." Had a teacher intervened, neither child would likely have so critically examined his own perspectives. The role of the teacher for Piaget is to foster changes in children's thinking by stimulating play, experimentation, and reasoning, and also by providing opportunities for children to collaborate socially (DeVries and Kohlberg 1987).

Internalizing Social Experiences

Like Piaget, Vygotsky (1978) describes learning as a *constructive* act. Both Piaget and Vygotsky believe that children construct knowledge through active and thoughtful engagement with their worlds (Neuman and Roskos 1993). Both believe that children learn by reorganizing new ideas to make them fit within their existing schemas. However, Vygotsky emphasizes the social nature of this process and, therefore, offers a different perspective on learning.

Vygotsky argues that the social use of language is a great contributor to children's learning. When children experience language, it is most often within the rich context of daily living. As they go about their daily lives, competent language users talk in childrens' presence, and talk with them, about a variety of things. As they talk, their actions often provide clues to the meaning of their language. In this way, language *mediates* action. Consider an example. Twelve-month-old Marybeth starts to fuss. Her mother puts her into a high chair, and says, "Marybeth's getting hungry. Let's get you something to eat. You're hungry, aren't you, Marybeth? Here, try some pasta." Later, Marybeth's sister, Rachel, helps Marybeth to her feet. Marybeth is on the verge of walking. Rachel says to her, "Come on, Marybeth, take a step. Step, Marybeth. Take a step . . . Mom! She took a step! She took a little one."

New capacities are developed as children interact socially and then transform the language and actions of their social experiences into tools for independent thinking. Transformation is not akin to copying, mimicking, or imitation. Transformation involves a process of *internalization* in which children select—and modify to meet their own needs—the communicative and problem-solving tools of the people around them. An example from a preschool classroom puts this into perspective:

Andrea: Mrs. Lee, I want to go in the house area.

Mrs. Lee: Well, how many people are in there?

Andrea: One, two.

Mrs. Lee: [*slowly counting, pointing to each child in the house area*] One . . . two . . . three. How many *can* be in there?

Andrea: Four.

Mrs. Lee: So, it looks like there's room for you!

In this scenario, Mrs. Lee mediates the social event with language and gesture (problem-solving tools), but it is up to Andrea to adjust and structure this feedback in a way that makes sense to her (Piaget 1952; Vygotsky 1978). This process of bringing information from the outside world to the inside does not involve a direct transmission of knowledge from adult to child. Rather, as knowledge moves from the external plane of the social world to the internal plane of the child, it is restructured and individualized based on the child's current understandings. Andrea will take only what she internalizes from her problem-solving transaction with Mrs. Lee to use as a future tool for her own thinking.

Vygotsky's *internalization* is comparable to Piaget's *assimilation* and *accommodation*. Both theories emphasize the notion that children restructure new experiences to make them adaptable to their existing schemas. Children build new concepts based upon what makes sense to them already. While both theories emphasize the importance of action and exploration, Vygotsky placed much more emphasis on the contributions that social experiences could make to knowledge construction.

Working Within the Zone of Proximal Development

For Vygotsky (1978), learning occurs within a child's *zone of proximal development*. The zone of proximal development can be thought of as an area in which children experience a challenge as they pursue a task, but do not become frustrated (Isenberg and Jalongo 1997). The zone is activated in two ways: through social collaboration and through children's play.

Social Collaboration

Consider the zone that is created by *social collaboration*. Vygotsky holds the position that learning involves being introduced—through language—to the symbolic world of adults. Knowledge is constructed through children's social involvement in talk, activity, and problem solving. When children engage in an activity on their own, they function at their *actual* level of development. With guidance (social problem solving), they are able to function at their *potential* level of development. The difference between the actual and the potential defines the zone of proximal development. In the example used earlier, Andrea was initially working by herself (at her actual level), but was unable to determine whether she could play in the house area. With guidance, her zone was activated and she moved toward her problem-solving potential.

The task of the developmentally appropriate teacher is to learn about individual children's zones. When we observe what children can do when their zones are activated, we know the direction they are going next in their development, and we can teach in this direction. "What is in the zone of proximal development today will be the actual developmental level tomorrow—that is, what a child can do with assistance today she will be able to do by herself tomorrow" (Vygotsky 1978, 87).

Play

Play, too, creates a zone of proximal development, even when children play by themselves. Play frees children to take risks and to explore roles that they are not yet fully equipped to fill in real life. "In play a child always behaves beyond his average age, above his daily behavior; in play it is as though he were a head taller than himself" (102). For example, children playing as bank tellers try to follow rules for bank tellers as they understand them. They use calculators, complex terms, and a form of businesslike language that is uncharacteristic of ordinary conversation. "What passes unnoticed by the child in real life becomes a rule of behavior in play" (9). In play, children explore more sophisticated ways of thinking and acting than they explore outside of play.

For Vygotsky, then, both social transactions and play bring children into their zones of proximal development. Both kindle mental functions that are in the process of developing, rather than those which have already developed. It is within the zone that children make connections between the known and the new, and internalize the problem-solving tools of their society. Therefore, the ultimate task of education is to support the kinds of experiences that help to activate children's zones. Let them engage in meaningful conversation, solve problems together, and play. In developmentally appropriate classrooms, "[w]hole group meetings or discussion times give children an opportunity to build a sense of community and shared purpose and to take part in group problem solving . . . Children have daily opportunities to learn with others through conversation during work or play" (Bredekamp and Copple 1997, 163). In classrooms, rarely does one adult activate the zone of one child at a time. Rather, all of the children within the social community activate zones all over the classroom as they play, talk, and share their understandings of the world.

The Role of Talk

As we have learned from Vygotsky, the social use of language is an important part of children's construction of knowledge. Vygotsky also believes children's *self*-talk to be facilitative of their development, observing that initially, "children solve practical tasks with the help of their speech, as well as their eyes and hands" (1978, 26). They use language to work their way through tasks, especially when the tasks are complex. "Sometimes speech becomes of such vital importance that, if not permitted to use it, young children cannot accomplish the given task" (26). As an example, consider the spelling efforts of my niece, Ivy, as she pretended to grade and write comments on her "students'" papers. Two of her comments were: "Try to remember you [are] a 3rd grader" and "Please Concentrate." As she wrote, I noticed that she quickly and effortlessly wrote words that she uses frequently, such as *to* and *you,* but as she wrote *concentrate* and *remember* (Figure 3–1), she furrowed her little brow and I could hear her whispering letters and sounds to herself.

According to Vygotsky, children use talk to organize their thinking and to help them work their way through difficult tasks. As they grow older, these external processes develop into internal mental functions. Vygotsky hypothesizes that self-talk (which sounds much the same as what Piaget referred to as egocentric speech) "should be regarded as the transitional form between external and internal speech" (27). It is a necessary part of children's development.

Piaget and Vygotsky hold differing views on the role of language in learning. To Vygotsky, language *contributes* to development, and is part of the cultural tool kit that helps children to organize their thinking and work out

Figure 3–1. Ivy's Comments to Her "Students"

solutions to complex problems. On the other hand, Piaget views language as a *reflection* of children's development, more like a by-product of their activity and exploration (Berk and Winsler 1995).

BRINGING THEORY INTO THE CLASSROOM

Although there are differences between Piaget's and Vygotsky's views on knowledge construction, both believe that internal and social forces contribute to the shaping of children's understandings. While Piaget emphasizes the internal processes that lead to knowledge construction, he acknowledges that teaching and social collaboration can support this process. While Vygotsky emphasizes the social influences on children's development, he acknowledges that challenges provided by the physical environment can help children to revise their thinking (Berk and Winsler 1995). Both theorists believe that children learn through active experiences in the environment and that these experiences must be adapted by children to make them fit with their current understandings.

Let's think about what *teaching* means when we weave together the ideas of Piaget and Vygotsky. We have seen that to learn is to build schemas through the processes of assimilation and accommodation. Assimilation and accommodation are the means by which children change and develop their working models of the world. Assimilation and accommodation are ways of adapting to new experiences, which, according to Piaget, is what learning is all about. Schema building is an internal process, so only learners know how they can adapt to a new piece of information at a given point in time. Piaget (1973) argues, therefore, that education must provide children with opportunities to engage in spontaneous action that takes its direction from the learners themselves. When we let children get their hands on things to tackle new ideas and hypotheses, we are supporting their natural processes of learning. We are giving them the opportunity to assimilate and accommodate and to let those internal processes come alive and grow.

Of course we don't leave everything up to the learners, knowing that the social part of learning is very important, too. Recall my grandmother's situation with computers and e-mail. If my grandmother decides that computers aren't so bad and chooses to get one, my family certainly won't leave it up to her to figure out on her own, and we certainly won't just *tell* her how to use it. Instead, we will let her show us what she needs. We might start by getting the computer all set up for her in a comfortable place. Then we might sit beside her when she first attempts to use it. We will take her lead as she explores, trying to provide instruction that is just beyond what she could do by herself. Does she turn on the computer? If not, we'll ask, "How do you think you might turn it on? Have you ever turned on anything like this before?" Does she press any keys? If not, we'll say, "What is that prompter telling you to do? . . . Yes, you clicked the mouse and got to a new screen." By using language to *mediate* the event, perhaps the next time she will use the terms *prompter* and *mouse* to guide her own thinking.

Although we are teaching, my grandmother will have to work out many things for herself. Knowledge cannot simply be transmitted from one person to another; we don't just take in what we are taught. We take it in and transform it, making it fit with our current understandings. For this reason, my grandmother's schema for e-mail will not be exactly like yours or mine. The shape of knowledge changes as it moves from the outside to the inside because it has to adapt to the schema that is already there. Therefore, when my grandmother talks about e-mail, we shouldn't be surprised if she demonstrates some unconventional understandings—or at least some conceptions that are quite different from our own.

Teaching in a developmentally appropriate way requires that teachers provide children with opportunities to explore and manipulate materials, make observations, reflect, ask questions, and develop hypotheses to answer these questions (Bredekamp and Copple 1997). "Constructing knowledge is the result of the learner's own action" (Ferreiro and Teberosky 1982, 15). Action that is overly planned or teacher-centered cannot adequately help children to build knowledge or make discoveries because it cannot bring about the kinds of thinking that allow them to build upon their unique schemas. Children make sense of new information based on their current levels of understanding and cannot be expected to do so in any other way (Hulit and Howard 1993). Therefore, as you facilitate children's learning in a developmentally appropriate classroom, you are:

- A planner and creator of an environment rich in opportunities for hands-on exploration. You provide materials that are neither too simple, nor too complex, but which seem just right for your children to seek answers to their many questions about the world.

- A supporter of social collaboration and problem solving among children. You understand that children learn from one another as they talk, share ideas, and play together. You are aware that conflicting viewpoints among children often induce the cognitive conflict that leads to new learning.

- A collaborator in problem solving. As you collaborate with children, you model the communicative and problem-solving tools of our society. You listen to children, and, taking their lead, make suggestions and provide insights from the adult perspective.

- An asker of questions. Your questions are aimed at stimulating children's reasoning and helping them to move a step forward in their thinking. Children are the constructors of their own knowledge. You support them by encouraging them to articulate and mentally organize their ideas.

- A listener. You know that self-talk and social talk are conducive to learning. If your children get a little vociferous, you simply shut the door so that they will not disturb others.

- An observer of children's zones of proximal development. By observing children as they collaborate socially, and as they play, you learn about the kinds of things they will be able to do on their own tomorrow. You teach toward their tomorrows.

- A facilitator of play. You know that play liberates children to take risks, to explore the worlds of their interests, and to learn about the perspectives and viewpoints of other people.

You teach in developmentally appropriate ways *for your children* because you value the knowledge they have developed already and because you trust in their ability to construct new knowledge. You do it *for their families* because you recognize and treasure what they have taught their children already and because you know that they want the best for their little ones. You do it *for yourself* because you know that to actively use your professional knowledge makes teaching the most challenging, stimulating, and rewarding endeavor you can imagine.

4

Children Construct Knowledge About Written Language

Aster: Amy, could you read this?

Amy: From Aster to Mom?

Aster: Yeah. My brother taught me how to write *from* and *to.*

Amy: You didn't know how to write *to?*

Aster: No.

Karla: No one had to teach me . . . I learned when I was two- or one-years-old.
No . . . I learned when I wasn't born yet.

Amy: I learned when I was in my mom's stomach.

Karla: I learned when I was in *my* mom's stomach.

Amy: I learned even before I was in my mom's stomach.

Karla: I did, too. I learned when I was in heaven.

Amy: I learned when I was nowhere.

With the charming ways of four- and five-year-olds, Aster, Amy, and Karla raise the issue that literacy knowledge is both internally and socially constructed. Some understandings seem to come from within, as if they have been there forever, while others can be helped along by a person—a big brother, for example. Aster, Amy, and Karla's ideas are quite on the mark. Children build schemas for written language just as they build schemas for everything else that is significant in their worlds (Ferreiro 1990; Goodman 1980, 1984). As they act on and explore the literate environment, they internally develop and test a never-ending series of hypotheses about the ways in which written language works. As social experiences challenge and inform their current ways of thinking, children modify their schemas to accommodate and assimilate the new information.

55

This chapter explores the major discoveries that children make as they build schemas for written language. Knowing about these discoveries and about how they are made is an essential part of facilitating literacy in developmentally appropriate ways. The more we know about children's development, the better able we are to provide instruction that is in tune with their needs. Although children do not develop at the same rate or in the same order, most make the following discoveries about language during the early childhood years:

- Written language serves a variety of functions.
- Written language takes a variety of forms.
- Written language has significant features.

Some of the most important discoveries they make about the features of written language are that:

- Print carries meaning.
- Written messages must correspond with oral language.
- Written symbols have conditions that make them interpretable.
- Graphic differences support different intentions.
- Letters and words are written in linear fashion.
- Written language is predictable.
- There is a relationship between letter patterns and sound patterns.
- Words have boundaries.

In 1998, the International Reading Association (IRA) and the National Association for the Education of Young Children (NAEYC) developed a joint position statement focusing on early literacy development. The statement, based on thirty years of research, reflects much of what is currently known about how children develop literacy. This position statement, along with many other works, supports our understanding of early literacy and helps us think about ways to best facilitate its development.

As early childhood professionals, we want to know about the functions of written language because children's knowledge of function provides the foundation for all future literacy exploration. When children know what written language can do for them, they want to use it, and they want to learn to use it conventionally so that it will meet their varied needs (Goodman 1986). If children do not understand that reading and writing serve important functions, then there is little reason for them to read or write. So, let's start by exploring how children learn about the functions of written language.

WRITTEN LANGUAGE SERVES A VARIETY OF FUNCTIONS

Three-year-old Juan Pablo is riding in the car with his mother. When they approach a STOP sign, Juan Pablo warns his mother, "Stop, Mama. You have to stop at STOP signs."

Ana and her four-year-old sister, Marisela, are making cookies.

Ana: [*reading from a cookbook*] Okay, one cup of sugar. Marisela, want to pour in the sugar?

Marisela: Yeah!

Ana: Now, what's next? . . . We need two eggs. Get the eggs out, Mari.

Five-year-old Nicole is in the cereal aisle at the grocery store. "Cereal's on the list, right Nana?" Nicole picks a colorful box of cereal from the shelf and hands it to her grandmother. "Here! I saw this one on TV!" "Wait," her grandmother says. "We can't get this one. Look, sugar is the first ingredient."

Written language is pervasive in our society. We use it to do many things. "For the majority of children in the Western world many encounters with literacy occur before school, often unrecorded and transient, but nevertheless powerful and cumulative in their effect" (Weinberger 1998, 39). As families engage in daily events such as running errands, watching television, going shopping, and preparing meals, they use written language to serve a variety of functions. In the vignettes, Juan Pablo and his mother use written language to guide their driving; Ana and Marisela use written language to put the right ingredients into their cookie dough and to find the necessary food packages; Nicole and her grandmother use written language to make a grocery list and to get information about the ingredients in foods. In a society geared to print, using written language to get things done is a natural and important part of living.

Building Schemas for Functions

Young children build schemas for the many functions that written language serves through their daily literacy experiences. For example, at the age of four, Marisela has already used recipes to make cookies, bread, and tortillas. With each new recipe, she assimilates information about what recipes are for, and eventually concludes that they are used for preparing all kinds of food. When something new challenges her existing schema, she accommodates the information to make it fit with what she knows. For example, when her sister brings home a recipe for play dough, Marisela accommodates. She creates a new schematic category for nonfood recipes and concludes that recipes serve more than one function. Children build schemas for the functions of written language by participating socially in a variety of everyday experiences.

Four Major Functions

Having a conscious awareness of the functions of written language helps the early childhood teacher to provide a balanced range of opportunities for meaningful exploration. A number of researchers (Goodman 1986; Halliday 1975; McGee and Richgels 1996; Schrader 1989; Whitmore and Goodman 1995) have identified ways of organizing the functions of language into sets of categories for use in the classroom. I prefer a broad, simple set that I can easily remember (and count on one hand). When I work with young children, a simple set of categories makes it easy to consider whether all of the functions are being explored. If they are not being explored I can quickly figure out which areas to improve. I find the following set of functions to be quite usable in the classroom: environmental, occupational, informational, and recreational (Goodman 1986, 1996; Whitmore and Goodman 1995). Sometimes, because a piece of written language can serve more than one function, it will fall into more than one of these categories. Sometimes it is difficult to determine which category a piece of written language fits into. Don't be concerned when the function seems ambiguous or when you can't decide; the point is to understand that written language serves many functions and to support children in exploring these functions as they play. As you read through the following definitions and examples, think about how you provide opportunities for their exploration during play time in your classroom:

- *Environmental Print* provides information about the world around us. Examples of environmental print can be found on street signs, store signs, book jackets, schedules, bills, price tags, and coupons; and, in advertisements, instructions, directories, and reference books.

- *Occupational Print* is used to do one's job. Children see occupational print in the workplace, and sometimes, in their homes. The occupational print for a dentist might include health records, patient progress sheets, reference materials, and appointment books. The occupational print for a waiter might be found on menus, order pads, signs, and money. Children, provided they have access to print materials, are likely to explore all kinds of occupational print as they take on a variety of play roles.

- *Informational Print* is for storing, organizing, and retrieving information. Examples of informational print can be found on calendars, clocks, diagrams, and receipts and in biographies, encyclopedias, newspapers, and telephone books. Informational print can also be found on health records, also listed under *occupational print,* showing that print often serves more than one function.

- *Recreational Print* is used for leisure activities. Examples of recreational print can be found in novels, storybooks, magazines, poetry books, movie critiques, television books, and travel books.

If you were to observe the children in your classroom for a thirty-minute play session, how many different functions would you see being explored? Would all of the above categories be covered? How many meaningful ways could you find to introduce new functions? What materials would be necessary? Asking yourself these questions will help you provide your children with opportunities to explore a broad range of functions as they play. Of course, the children can explore these functions in nonplay activities, but we want them to have the opportunity to explore them through play as well, knowing that play frees children to try out ideas that they may not try otherwise (Vygotsky 1978).

As the children in Curt Kiwak and Trish Hill's classroom engage in restaurant play, they explore the functions of *environmental* print because they have access to examples of advertisements, signs, and coupons, and because they have access to the materials they need to create these objects. They explore *occupational* print as they read menus, take food orders, and read food packages. They explore *informational* print as they prepare receipts. They may even explore *recreational* print if they bring a good book or magazine to peruse while waiting for their food to be prepared.

If no print is brought into the play, Curt or Trish may make a literacy-related suggestion or model a use of written language: "Do you want a menu?" "Do you need some paper to write down that order?" "What do I want to order? Let me see, I think I'll need a menu." Curt and Trish always model and suggest uses of written language based on the children's existing play themes. This keeps play in the hands of the children and helps them understand why a use of written language in a particular situation makes sense. Of course, Curt and Trish don't do all of the teaching; their children model for one another many functional uses of written language.

The Origin of Understandings About Function

As we have seen, children's schemas for the functions of written language are initially shaped by the literacy events that occur in the home. Children develop very different understandings about written language depending on the amount of talk surrounding these events, the degree of literacy in the environment, and family values and attitudes about literacy (Goodman 1984). By the time they come to school, then, children can be expected to have a diversity of knowledge about the functions of written language. Some will have been included in many literacy experiences while others will have experienced literacy from the sidelines. Some will have talked often about print while others will rarely have had this opportunity. Some will see written language as a useful thing while others will hardly be aware of its presence. Your goal, therefore, is to find ways for your children to build knowledge based on the functions they know already, and at the same time to explore new functions. The following suggestions can help you:

- Develop a conscious knowledge of the functions of written language so that you know whether you are supporting a balanced variety of exploration.
- Ensure that your children have access to a variety of literacy materials as they play; let them expand upon what they know already.
- Observe play, looking for meaningful ways to model and suggest exploration of functions.
- Deliberately model uses of written language throughout the school day. For example, point out what you are doing when you use a recipe to make play dough or trail mix with your children; if you keep a calendar in the classroom, deliberately show the children how you use it; or, if you take attendance, invite the children to participate.

By actively participating in a variety of literacy events, children learn a great deal about the functions of written language. Play is a powerful medium for discovering functions because it engenders so many good reasons to read and write. As children discover the many functions of written language in a supportive, print-rich environment, they also construct knowledge about its *forms*.

WRITTEN LANGUAGE TAKES A VARIETY OF FORMS

Four-year-old Karla is playing as a waitress. She points to the menu that her customer is holding and tells him, "That—well, this is the drink side, and this is the dessert and dinner side."

Form (or format) is the "shape," or configuration, that written language takes when it is used to serve a specific purpose. For example, the food choices in a menu are often presented in sections (drinks, entrees, desserts), and are accompanied by prices and short descriptions. The format depends on the function that written language is intended to serve. Restaurant patrons need simple, clear descriptions, and they need prices. These needs shape the format that written language takes in a menu.

As we saw earlier, the children in Curt's classroom have many opportunities to explore the functions of written language. Because they play in a literacy-rich environment, they also have opportunities to explore its forms. For example, the literacy props in their play restaurant enable them to explore the organization of language in menus, on signs, on cash registers, and on receipts. Karla is not yet reading conventionally, but having a menu as a play prop helps her explore the forms that written language takes in a menu. Nor is she writing conventionally, but having an order pad and a pencil helps her explore the form that written language takes when it is used to remember a list of items. As she uses and talks about written language, she is sharing her knowledge with her friends. As children explore and socially experience the use of a variety of literacy materials, they build schemas for the many functions and forms of written language.

Genre Is Related to Form

Genre is closely related to form. Examples of genres include fairy tales, fables, adventure stories, instruction manuals, invitations, recipes, and notes. A genre is a category of language that is used to classify its *form* and *content.* For example, restaurant workers take food orders by writing lists. A list is the form; the names of the food are the content. A restaurant order could be considered a genre. Genre takes its shape depending on the purposes of the writer and the needs of the audience—the functions the written language is intended to serve. One audience for a restaurant order is the chef, who needs just a brief list to know what food to prepare. A list is an appropriate format for taking a restaurant order because it is efficient and includes all of the necessary information. Knowledge of various genres helps writers form clear, efficient messages without expending a lot of energy deciding how to organize their writing.

Knowledge of genre is extremely important for readers, too, because it is used to make meaning from text (Pappas and Pettigrew 1998). The more children know about what to expect in a piece of writing in terms of form and content, the easier it is to predict and interpret its meaning. A five-year-old "chef" is going to read a food order, knowing that the writing is in the form of a list of related words and knowing that the list contains foods makes it easier for him to read. This knowledge helps narrow the possibilities for what the words could be.

Story Genre

> Karla is sitting at the writing table with her friend, Angie. She is writing a story using letterlike symbols. She reads aloud what she has written so far: "One morning, three curious cats and dogs got tooken to a wonderful place called animal control. They all got tooken in cages that early morning in the summer . . ."

Story is an important genre to discover during the early childhood years. Stories help children learn about and make sense of the world. Through stories, children experience imaginative ideas, new possibilities for doing things, and diverse ways of thinking and living. Stories are fun to read. They are fun to share. And they are the major source of text used to facilitate literacy in early childhood classrooms.

Children build schemas for the language and elements of stories as they listen to and talk about books and as they write in a social community. As they engage in these activities, they discover that stories are made up of characters, settings, problems, and resolutions. They learn that particular stories involve particular events. For example, a folktale is a type of story that is usually based on a plot involving only one problem and is often resolved with magic, spells, or wishes. The characters in folktales are often stereotypical (foxes are clever; wolves are deceptive) and the themes are predictable (the poor get rich; the ugly gain beauty; the good triumph over the evil) (Raines and Isbell 1994). Familiarity with these story elements makes decoding and interpreting story text easier for children. They know what to expect when they read, and these expectations make their processing of information easier.

Karla, in writing her story about animal control, demonstrates a sophisticated knowledge of the story genre. The first two lines of her story are filled with literary conventions. First, she begins with "One morning," a typical story beginning. Second, she introduces the characters right at the beginning, just like many authors do. Third, Karla gives some information about the setting: she refers to animal control as a "wonderful place." From the perspective of the animals, it probably is a wonderful place, because animal-control agencies often remove animals from abusive homes. Fourth, Karla sets up an initiating event—going to animal control—which suggests that there has been a problem for the protagonists—another story convention. Fifth, Karla's language sounds like story language, not the typical conversational language of a four-year-old. She uses the terms "wonderful" and "curious" and "that early morning in the summer." Karla is gaining good practice at fictionalizing real-life events.

Karla knows about story genre because she has listened to many stories, and has begun to make up and write stories of her own. As she continues to develop conventional understandings about reading and writing, she will have some very useful understandings to support her. For example, as she begins to use alphabet letters and pay attention to sounds while writing stories, she will not need to expend much effort thinking about how stories are organized and she will certainly not be under the impression that she has nothing interesting to write. Karla is coming to see herself as an author.

Symbolic play is another way of developing understandings about story (Hall 1998). As children play, they often create story lines which include characters, settings, problems, and resolutions. Consider the story elements included in the following vignette, in which monsters Angie and Todd are preparing for a royal monster-wedding. Karla, a monster-princess, is helping with the preparations:

Angie: [*to Todd*] Pretend when I arrived you were where you were supposed to be, and I wasn't where you were supposed to be. I was supposed to be right there. For the wedding.

Todd: And I died . . .

Angie: No, you didn't. When I was married to you, then you died, but it was after I had a baby.

Angie puts on a wedding dress and fastens a veil to her head.

Angie: Todd, pretend I put this on.

Karla: Yeah, and then you guys had your wedding.

Angie: [*to Karla*] Yeah, and I was marrying and I was queen of all monsters, and you were princess of all monsters . . .

Chloe: This is our monster-house. We're monsters.

In negotiating their play, Angie, Todd, Karla, and Chloe create characters (monsters), a setting (a monster-house), and some major story events (a wedding, a death, and the birth of a baby). Children's carrying out of story lines through their symbolic play helps them to explore the structure and meanings of stories, and provides a foundation for moving into putting stories on paper (Hall 1998).

Expository Genre

Colin (age 5) and Bowen (age 4) are pretending to be on a rocket ship in outer space. "Okay," says Colin, "let's read about Saturn [*pretending to read*]. It's made out of gravity, and rocks and sand. Saturn's the only planet that has rings."

Reading *expository text,* too, is an important part of children's early literacy development. Knowing about the ways in which expository text is organized (knowing about its form) facilitates children's ability to learn from this kind of writing (Barr and Johnson 1997) and makes their reading easier. Depending on their purposes, authors of expository text frequently choose from a set of text structures, such as cause and effect, problem and resolution, comparison and contrast, definition and example, or time-order. When children have expectations about these forms, they can anticipate what is coming next in their reading and can mentally prepare to assimilate the information. For example, if they read a comparison, they ready themselves for a contrast; if they read a definition, they ready themselves for an example. Knowing about text structure helps children to organize their schemas to process new information. If the text form is confusing or unfamiliar, children may have to reread several times before getting the gist of the passage.

Children build schemas for text structures as well as for the content of expository text as they look through books, share in their reading, and create their own pieces of writing. Colin has obviously experienced this kind of writing before. He knows about the kind of information to expect in the text and he knows that it will be full of factual information. The more experience children have with expository text, the easier it becomes to learn from it.

There may be children in your classroom who take a great interest in expository text, making this genre a potentially important avenue into their literacy. Their interest can make reading seem more worthwhile, it may lead to more active, persistent reading and writing, and expository text may be more in tune than story genres with the literacy the child is experiencing in the home (Caswell and Duke 1998). And, of course, we learn important facts and information from exposition that we may not learn from other kinds of text.

Children Learn to Take a Stance

As children explore a variety of genres, they learn to take a *stance* (Rosenblatt 1991) or to set a purpose for reading. The stance taken influences the way that the reading is approached, and therefore, the meaning that is constructed. Taking a stance, like having an expectation for form and content, readies the mind for assimilating new information. Colin and Bowen took a predominantly *efferent* stance in their pretend reading about Saturn: they focused on obtaining information that they could carry away from the experience. According to Rosenblatt, the efferent stance usually predominates in the reading of textbooks, recipes, or scientific reports. Colin and Bowen's efferent stance is context-appropriate: they were reading nonfictional materials, seeking information about outer space. Although neither child visibly attended to the print, both explored the possibilities for the kind of language and information that could be found in expository text.

Karla, on the other hand, in reading her story about animal control, took a predominantly *aesthetic* stance. When readers take an aesthetic stance, they focus on what they are seeing, feeling, and thinking, making more personal connections than when taking an efferent stance (Rosenblatt 1991).

According to Rosenblatt, every reading event falls somewhere along the continuum between the efferent and the aesthetic. Stance is determined by the reader within the context of each reading event. Mature readers automatically select a stance that is appropriate to their needs, but this act of "selective attention" must be learned by children. Karla, Colin, and Bowen show that four- and five-year-olds explore stances in their play, and that they are able to choose stances that are appropriate to the context of their play themes.

In Support of Literacy Development

As an early childhood teacher, you can help children take stances, and expand their knowledge of the forms and genres of written language in the following ways:

- Share in the reading of all kinds of books, talking with children about literary elements (Which character did you like? Would you have solved the problem in the same way?) and text structures (Where could we find out about Saturn? Are there any examples?). Although reading may not always be a part of dramatic play themes, many children choose books during play time. Therefore, a variety of literature should be available to children during play.

- Help children to take a stance by discussing with them their purposes for reading and helping them set purposes when their approach seems vague.

- Observe children's play to see whether they are exploring a variety of forms and genres of written language. Do the materials in the play environment lend themselves to exploration of form and genre? If not, find materials to facilitate this exploration.

- Enter children's play with the intention of modeling real-life uses of written language. Talk with children about what you are writing and reading, deliberately stating your purposes and modeling the use of different organizational styles.

Knowledge of the forms and functions of written language allows children to participate in the literate community, even if they are not yet conventional in their understandings of print. When you purposefully include children in daily literacy events, when you provide print-filled opportunities for play, and when you share with them a variety of literature, you help them to participate in the world of literacy and to develop a strong foundation for literacy.

WRITTEN LANGUAGE HAS SIGNIFICANT FEATURES

"Knowledge of the forms and functions of print serves as a foundation from which children become increasingly sensitive to letter shapes, names, sounds, and words" (IRA/NAEYC 1998, 35). Another major benefit of helping children to expand their knowledge of functions and forms is that it leads to exploration of features—letter-sound relationships, grammatical structures, and the meanings that are embedded within written language.

Print Carries Meaning

Two-year-old Chloe is sorting through a stack of books. Her teacher, Trish, is sitting nearby.

Chloe: Can you read me a book?

Trish: Sure. Which one do you want me to read first?

Chloe opens a book which contains photographs of paintings, but only a small amount of writing.

Chloe: It's a looking-book.

Trish: It's a looking-book. Not a storybook.

One of the earliest discoveries children make about the features of written language is that print carries meaning. The little symbols that we call letters are much more than little shapes or designs; they actually say something. At the age of two, Chloe has made this discovery. She knows that print must be present if her teacher is to read her a story. If we want to know whether children view print as something meaningful, we have to observe them attentively, because when print is embedded in a real-life context, there are often other clues to its meaning. For example, a chocolate-chip cookie package may be decorated with pictures of cookies, or, perhaps the Os in the word *Cookies* are presented as round shapes which resemble cookies. Ask any child what the package says, and the response almost always will be "cookies." Ask which part of the package says "cookies," and some will point to the pictures, some to the words. We can learn whether children understand that print is meaningful by asking, "How do you know what that says?" or "Where does it say *cookies?*" or "Can you show me where I am [you are] reading?" (Goodman 1983).

We can also determine whether children understand that print carries meaning by observing them as they make marks on paper. Figure 4–1 shows Katie's writing of her friend Chloe's name. Katie shows her understanding that print carries meaning . . . even though her writing looks like scribbling. We can't know whether young children have developed the understanding that

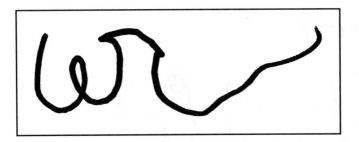

Figure 4–1. Katie's Writing of Chloe's Name

print carries meaning unless we observe them as they write and/or talk with them about their written products.

Katie's writing system is like that of many beginners. Although she has not yet begun to write letters, she uses a cursive style to communicate something. Ferreiro and Teberosky (1982) distinguish between early cursive writing, "graphic characters—closed or open curves—linked together by a wavy line," and early printing, "separate graphic characters composed of curved and/or straight lines" (180). Although early forms of cursive and print may not be conventional, we can call them writing because they are intended to communicate something.

Karla used invented print symbols (see Figure 4–2) to plan for play one day at preschool. The knowledge Karla demonstrates about written language becomes apparent by observing her write and by talking with her about her written product. After writing seven lines of symbols, she read them aloud as "housekeeping." Then she announced, "I'm also going to play with the rat." She then wrote two more lines of symbols while saying, " *Rat. Rat.* See, like *rat* almost. Just like a few more words. *Rat.* Now, I'm going to make a picture of a rat." She finished her plan by drawing a rat and a picture of the housekeeping area on her page. Although Karla is far from conventional in her writing, she shows an awareness that print is different from drawing, and that written symbols actually mean something. She also understands that written language can help her plan her playtime activities.

Print Is a Close Representation of Objects

As they are discovering that print carries meaning, some children hypothesize that print is used only to *label* objects; in other words, print can represent an object, but can not describe it or tell what it does (Ferreiro and Teberosky 1982). Many children do not pay much attention to the graphic characteristics of print when they first begin to assign it a label. For example, LaWanda

Figure 4–2. Karla's Plan for Play

read the writing on a chart containing a picture of a flying bat as just "bat," even though she was referring to five lines of print. Marguerite read the brand name on a box of raisin bran as "cereal." In making her plan for play, Karla used print as a label for *rat,* and also for *housekeeping.* It is interesting that, early on, many children expect print to contain only the name of what is in the picture, but no other words. For example, Karla did not read her text as "the housekeeping area" or "the rat," although she used *the* in her talk; instead, she dropped the article when she moved from talk to writing.

Some children may assign a whole sentence (as opposed to a label) to text. However, as with labeling, they do not pay attention to the graphic characteristics of the text. In both cases, the child's conceptualization of what can be written remains relatively close to the physical object they are trying to represent. For example, when a picture is present, children are likely to describe what is in the picture, rather than hypothesizing that the text could say something like, "On the following day, the dog . . ." Ferreiro and Teberosky (1982) note that there are midpoints between assigning a label and assigning a sentence. For example, when asked to read a line of text, a child at a midpoint might say, "Dog running," or "Dog went for a walk."

Ferreiro and Teberosky suggest that children's assignment of meaning to text, even though they are not attending to its graphic characteristics, is an important phase in their literacy development; it shows a differentiation between text and picture and is a first step toward sorting out the meaning of print.

In Support of Literacy Development

To facilitate children's understanding that print carries meaning, you

- Use print in the presence of children and talk with them about what it says.
- Read aloud to children, drawing their attention to the print. Occasionally point to words as you read, and point out and discuss individual words and phrases.
- Establish a literacy-rich play environment. Children who are exposed to written language in a variety of contexts (not just through books) make connections between print and its meanings.
- Ask questions such as "What do you think that says?" This gives you an idea of children's concepts about print and therefore helps you to provide instruction that suits their developmental needs.
- Provide opportunities for children to draw and experiment with writing (IRA/NAEYC 1998). Ask them to read what they have written.

Many children do not at first attend to the graphic characteristics of print, but are willing, nonetheless, to assign it meaning. We look in the following sections at some of the hypotheses that children may test when they start paying attention to the graphic characteristics of print. Because children take such different routes to literacy, the presentation of hypotheses should be considered only roughly sequential.

Written Messages Must Correspond with Oral Language

Karla is using invented print symbols to take a restaurant order. She writes four lines of symbols, and then reads them aloud, pointing to the words, and pausing between each line of print: "Eggs and . . . Bacon and . . . Sal- . . . ad" (Figure 4–3).

Soon after discovering that print carries meaning, children begin to hypothesize about the ways in which print is organized. Karla is doing that. As she reads what she has written, she shows an appreciation for the fact that her oral language must match with her written message. She writes four lines of print and then forces her oral language to match those lines. To leave a line of print hanging would leave her in a state of cognitive conflict (Ferreiro and Teberosky 1982). Although Karla is not yet conventional in her writing or reading, her temporary hypothesis helps her to maintain a sense of equilibrium as she works her way toward conventional understandings.

Written Symbols Have Conditions
That Make Them Interpretable

Brian finishes writing a book full of pictures and invented cursive. "Look at my book," he announces to his friends. "It's neato. Look how many pages there are. It's a boring book, you know why? You know why it's so boring? Because it's—sometimes it's—it's just waves. But, I don't know how to make the letters, so I just write waves."

At some point during the early childhood years, children begin to hypothesize that there is a difference between pretend and real reading and writing; they recognize that some strings of letters (including those in their own writing) are not readable, although they may have not yet discovered the actual criteria that makes something readable (Ferreiro 1990). They come to know that they are pretending while reading and writing, but still like to do it. Brian demonstrates his awareness that he is not writing conventionally, but his inventions provide a way for him to sort out his current understandings. He will soon begin to look for the conditions that make written symbols interpretable, if he is not doing so already.

Figure 4–3. Karla's Restaurant Order

Graphic Differences Support Different Intentions

Many children initially attempt to use the same letter string to represent two different objects or ideas. Consider the following example, in which four-year-old Carlos writes a sign (using invented characters) as his teacher, Peter, observes:

Carlos: [*reading from his sign*] "No Girls Allowed In My Bedroom."

Peter: Does that mean your mom's not going to come in?

Carlos: It says "No Girls Allowed Except My Mom."

Carlos is satisfied that he has changed what his sign says by changing the meaning in his mind. Eventually, children discover that in order to represent two different objects, the letters in a string must vary.

When children make this discovery, they actively begin to seek out graphic differences in strings of letters that will support their different intentions. They may look for both *quantitative* and *qualitative* ways to represent these differences (Ferreiro and Teberosky 1982). Initial quantitative attempts might be, for example, to use long strings of letters to represent big things (house) and shorter strings to represent small things (wagon); or, to use large print to represent big things, and small print to represent small things.

Qualitatively, children may try to represent different objects by using different strings of letters or by changing a few of the letters in one word to make it represent another word. For example, Erin wrote E-R-I-H-H-D for *bottle* and then E-R-I-H-C-D for *portrait.* She changed a few letters with the intent of changing the meaning. Or children may try changing the linear order of their letters. For example, Aster wrote three words on her paper, and then read them aloud to her teacher:

WRITTEN	READ ALOUD
P R i W	Pencil
R P i	Paper
P E i O	Envelope

Both Aster and Erin are beginning to use graphic differences to represent their different intentions. As with many children, their current stock of graphic letter forms is limited, so they use the same letters over and over but change their linear order to make them represent different meanings. Erin, like many young children, uses many of the letters in her name in each new word she invents.

In Support of Literacy Development

You can support children's early testing of hypotheses about written language by

- Making available for exploration a variety of print materials (IRA / NAEYC 1998).
- Giving children daily opportunities to write and try out their quantitative and qualitative hypotheses.
- Appreciating children's unconventional attempts at reading and writing. Teachers who "do not allow errors to occur . . . do not allow children to think." (Ferreiro and Teberosky 1982, 218).
- Giving children opportunities to use print in play and to collaborate in problem solving with peers so that they can make the challenges that lead to cognitive conflict, and thus, new learning.

- Encouraging children to talk about reading and writing (IRA/NAEYC 1998).
- Carefully observing children's writing and reading. Knowing where children are in their thinking enables you to support them based on their current levels of development.

Letters and Words Are Written in Linear Fashion

As children are busy exploring the functions, forms, and meanings of print, they are also learning about its directionality. As adults, we automatically know to read and write (in the English language) from left to right, and from top to bottom. Knowledge about directionality is not so obvious to children. Many children, when they are writing, scatter letters and words randomly about the page, or proceed in zigzag patterns. When they finger-point while pretending to read, they may use zigzag patterns, or even start at the bottom and move up. Developing directionality requires that children see others engaged in reading accompanied by specific gestures (Ferreiro and Teberosky 1982) such as finger pointing and page turning, and that they see others engaged in the act of writing. When families and teachers read (and write) with children and help them to focus their attention on words as well as illustrations, children begin to develop a sense of linearity (Bear and Barone 1998).

You help children to learn about the directionality of print by

- Occasionally pointing to words as you read, provided the pointing does not detract from the purpose of the literacy event.
- Modeling writing. Children notice the directionality of print when literate others model writing in their presence. Taking dictation is a good way to model linearity.

Written Language Is Predictable

When children notice that print carries meaning, they begin to make predictions about its meanings. *Predicting* is making an educated guess about what print says. For example, when I asked Heather, a first grader, to read a letter a friend of hers had written to a spider, she said, "'To—' I mean, 'Dear Spider . . .'" Without looking at the text, she could make an educated guess about what the print might say. Because children are users of language, they bring to each reading event certain expectations (predictions) about language that support their ability to make sense of text (Goodman 1996).

Let's look more closely at how prediction works. Read the following sentence and see if you can predict what might go in the blank: My big yellow dog gave me a big, slurpy _____. Before you actually connect your eyes with what goes in the blank space, you may have considerable knowledge about what it says. Because you know about the structure of language, you chose a noun; because you know about the meaning of language, you chose something that a dog can give. Using your deductive facilities, you may have guessed that the missing word is *kiss*. Can you see how predicting while reading makes the process efficient? If we are predicting, we need only sample the text with our eyes, rather than spending a lot of time decoding each word. A quick confirmation is all that is needed to establish that the word does indeed say *kiss*.

An example from a four-year-old at play that will help us consider in more detail how predicting helps readers.

> Curt and Aster are looking at an eye chart from a doctor's kit. Curt points to the progressively smaller letters which are used to test eyesight, and muses, "I wonder why all these letters are up there." Aster responds, "I think it says 'doctor kit.'"

Aster is willing to take the risk of prediction. She knows how to use cues from the situational context (playing with a doctor's kit), and from the pictures on the chart, to inform her prediction. Because she has seen and talked about written language in meaningful situations many times before, she knows how to make reasonable predictions. As she grows more sophisticated in her understandings, she will become more proficient at using the cues *within* the text to confirm or disconfirm her predictions. Readers use three types of in-text cues to make sense of print: graphophonic, syntactic, and semantic (Goodman 1996).

The *graphophonic* system deals with letter-sound relationships. If Aster had been using the graphophonic cueing system, she may have noted that the chart began with the letter *E* and that the letter *E* represents a certain category of sounds, but not the sound at the beginning of *doctor kit*. This may have helped her to disconfirm her initial prediction. Disconfirming and confirming predictions are important reading strategies because they help readers to connect what they expect to see with what is actually on the page. Aster, however, has not yet begun to make use of letter-sound relationships as she reads.

Aster's prediction does show her understanding of the other two cueing systems. The *syntactic* cueing system has to do with making predictions about language structure. Aster has a strong expectation of what the structure of the language on a sign in a doctor's kit might sound like. She has hypothesized that the letters might be a label—*doctor kit*—probably because she has experienced the use of such labels before. (Or, perhaps it is because she is hypothesizing that print can only be used to label things.)

The *semantic* cueing system has to do with making predictions about meaning. Aster is using the semantic cueing system as she makes a prediction about the content of the sign. She understands that there is a limited number of possibilities for what the sign could say. She knows that doctors have kits and that it would make sense for this piece of paper in this kit to say "doctor kit."

Aster's ability to make syntactic and semantic predictions will make her future reading easier; predictions narrow the range of possibilities for what the text might say. Readers continually make predictions and inferences about the semantic and syntactic content of what they are reading. As they read, they confirm and disconfirm their predictions based on the meaning they are making and based on the graphic cues in the text. Using all three systems in a balanced way frees the reader from relying too heavily on the graphophonic cues in the text. Therefore, teachers who emphasize sounding out words when children are stuck on a word, or who simply tell children unknown words, are not facilitating their ability to use a variety of reading strategies. Children learn more when we ask, "What would make sense?" "What sounds right?" and "Can the first letter of the word help?"

Through her play, Aster is exploring strategies and cues that are necessary for successful reading. Play is invaluable in this sense, because it provides a meaningful context and familiar ground for taking the risks that are necessary for trying out predictions. As Aster begins to negotiate the simultaneous use of all three cueing systems, these early experiences will make the process simpler. Aster's example shows that even before children are aware of letter-sound relationships, they are beginning to develop the ability to use the cueing systems that are used by proficient readers.

In Support of Literacy Development

To facilitate children's ability to predict, you can

- Encourage them to explore a variety of written language genres as they play. Familiarity with a variety of genres makes prediction in those genres easier.
- Ask questions such as "What do you think it says?" "What makes you think it says that?" "What could this word be?" "What would make sense here?"
- Demonstrate and model predicting as a reading strategy. For example, while reading a menu, you might say, "Let's see. We know we are reading in the drink section, and we know that this starts with a C. What could the word be? What are some drinks that starts with C?"
- Help children to think about their audience as they write. Working at making something predictable for an audience helps writers to develop their own predicting competency.

There Is a Relationship Between Letter Patterns and Sound Patterns

Harry writes M-O-M.

Harry: That spells *mom*, I think.

Karla: If that's the way you *think* you spell *mom*, then *spell mom*.

Harry: You know what? I think that's really how you spell *mom*. You know why? Because at kindergarten today we had to spell *mom*, and I think I remember how to spell *mom*. M-O-M. Mah . . . oh . . . mom.

Families and teachers delight when children find a way to control the phonetization of written symbols. Being able to connect letters with sounds is a major step toward being able to communicate with others through reading and writing. Like Harry, many children use their own names and the names of the people they know as they begin to hypothesize rationales for the ways in which letter strings are organized and as they begin to search for specific letters to represent specific sounds in words (Ferreiro and Teberosky 1982; Whitmore and Goodman 1995).

Syllabic and Alphabetic Hypotheses

Some children explore a *syllabic hypothesis* on their way to developing an understanding of the relationships between letter patterns and sound patterns. In other words, they hypothesize that a spoken syllable corresponds with each letter in a piece of writing (Ferreiro and Teberosky 1982). For example, when her teacher asked the class to put their journals away, Erin wrote a final note to herself:

Written:	O	Y	R	i
Spoken:	Put	away	jour	nals

Erin used one letter to represent each syllable in her writing. Some of her letters (*Y* for *away*; *R* for *jour-*) may indicate that she is becoming *alphabetic*, or, that she is discovering the relationships between letters and sounds, but the others (*O* for *put*; *I* for *nals*) do not seem to reflect this awareness. Erin's example illustrates that children exploring a syllabic hypothesis may or may not have knowledge about the precise letter with which the sound of the syllable begins.

In fact, children exploring a syllabic hypothesis need not be at all familiar with conventional letter formation. Karla drew a buckle on an envelope, and then wrote an invented symbol for each spoken syllable: "Un-buck-le-it-on-East-er. From Kar-la."

Many children exploring a syllabic hypothesis begin to use some letters to stand for syllables while others may be used to stand for smaller units of sound (Ferreiro and Teberosky 1982). After four-year-old Piper's mother read her the book *Lilly's Purple Plastic Purse* (Henkes 1996), Piper wrote her own version of a note that had been written by the main character of the book (Figure 4–4). The text from the book read, "BIG FAT MEAN MR. STEAL-ING TEACHER! WANTED BY THE F.B.I." Piper wrote and then read her own writing aloud as "Big fat mean Mr. Slinger! Entered by the F.B.I."

Figure 4–4. Piper's Response to a Book

Some of Piper's letters stand for syllables, such as *B* for *big* and *F* for *fat,* while others stand for smaller units of sound, as in *SLER* for *Slinger.* Piper is exploring both a syllabic and an alphabetic hypothesis.

Spelling Development

Throughout the early childhood years, children continually refine their alphabetic hypotheses as they interact with conventional text, and as they read and write in a social community. The series of discoveries they make can be observed through their writing. Early on, they may write words or syllables using only their most prominent sounds—often these are consonants. Piper's *B* for *big* and *F* for *fat* illustrate this principle. Children often include only the initial consonant (as in *L* for *like*), or the initial and final consonant (as in *LK* for *like*) before they begin to include the vowel sounds (as in *Lik*). Vowel markers, used when two vowels need to work together to make a certain sound (as in *like*), are typically discovered later (Wilde 1992).

Like any kind of language, spelling does not emerge in its conventional form. Children discover how to spell as they read, write, and receive feedback from others. Therefore, it is essential that we not become overly concerned with correcting children's inventions. Adults who put red marks or circles on children's spelling inventions may create writers who are afraid to take risks. When I began to teach, I required convention and my children often produced stories like the following: "I like a cat. It is good. I see it. It is nice." No red marks! When children are freed to invent, they are more apt to write stories like that written by Amy, a kindergartner in Curt Kiwak's classroom:

THE ERYR PLYN	The Airplane
DiW YOU WIT TO	Do you want to
TOYK ROYD	take a ride?
NO I WNT TO B IN	No, I want to be in
MY IRY PYN	my airplane.
R IRY PYN IS BIGIR	Our airplane is bigger.
YUIR IRY PYN	Your airplane
IS NOYSI	is noisy.
I DIN LIYK NWS SIF	I don't like noisy stuff.
BY BY	Bye-bye.
Im LY VN	I'm leaving.
Bic HWM NIYS	Back home. Nice.
NiW i KD NIP	Now I could nap.

Risk taking is an essential part of hypothesis testing, but it is fragile and can easily be damaged (Harste, Burke, and Woodward 1981). This means that children must be fully supported in their risk taking with spelling. We must let children invent so that they can sort out their current understandings. "Inventing is not so much an approach to writing as it is a way of removing obstacles in the path of a young writer" (Sowers 1991, 184).

Because children's development is somewhat predictable, we can look for signs that children have begun to follow a spelling rule or principle and then deliberately help them to extend what they know. First, this ensures that the children are conceptually ready to learn that rule or principle, and second, it allows them to build new principles from a place of familiarity. Often, several children will be making similar discoveries at the same time, and in small groups, you can work with them on particular patterns or strategies.

In Support of Literacy Development

To support children as they develop understandings about the relationships between letter patterns and sound patterns, you

- Surround children with all kinds of print in its real-life contexts. Children do not become confused when we teach letters and sounds in context (as opposed to isolating them). They sort out everything else in their worlds when it is in its real-life context. Why not written language?
- Facilitate children's ability to manipulate sounds by sharing poems, songs, fingerplays, and stories with rhyming or alliterative patterns (IRA/NAEYC 1998).
- Play language games with children (see Chapter 5).
- Give children time to write each day.
- Support children as they sound out words. Ask What do you think it starts with? Listen to me say the word. Do you hear any other sounds? You can ask older children to think about irregular spellings, prefixes, suffixes, base words, and vowel markers.
- Take dictation of children's writing and encourage them to read and reread what you have written.
- Make available a collection of familiar words from the environment. For example, ask all of the children in your class to cut words they can read from food package labels.
- Make available tapes of stories and expository text. Provide copies of the books so that children can follow along.

- Make charts with children of fun or interesting words. For example, make lists of color words, names, action words, rhyming words, words that sound like their meaning, words that contain similar vowel patterns, or words that begin with the same letter.
- Invite your children to make alphabet books or posters.
- Provide opportunities for social collaboration.

Words Have Boundaries

At some time, children discover that words in oral and written language have boundaries. While in oral language, strings of words are given meaning by influences such as pauses, intonation, the situational context, and nonverbal communication, in written language, spacing and punctuation serve these functions (Martens and Goodman 1996). Many children invent a temporary system for spacing, inserting periods, slashes, commas, or dashes between words before they develop the conventional form. Piper, in writing about "big, fat, mean Mr. Slinger," shows that she may be in the process of sorting out the concept of *word*. While most of her letters are right next to one another, she does have two distinguishable words (*oops* and *F.B.I.*). In order to space appropriately, children must know word segments as well as the function of a space (Clay 1975).

In Support of Literacy Development

To facilitate children's understandings about the concept of word, you

- Talk with children about environmental print. Often, environmental print contains isolated words.
- Encourage children to write. As they write, they experiment with spacing and eventually sort out its properties.
- Encourage children to watch as you write down what they say. This helps them see the connection between spoken words and written symbols.
- Point to words as you read. Ask children to point to words as you engage in shared readings.
- Encourage children to play with oral language (see Chapter 5).

These are some of the most important literacy discoveries that children make during the early childhood years. Teaching in a developmentally appropriate way is no easy task, but based on what we know about development, it is the only way of teaching that really makes any sense.

CONCLUSION

Knowing about the functions of written language empowers children to expand their knowledge about its forms, genres, and features. As children play in the roles of restaurant workers, chefs, pediatricians, post office workers, grandmothers, grocers, and authors, they experiment with the kinds of written language that they expect these individuals to use. As children experiment with written language they find out about its properties and sort out its rules. By engaging in a diversity of play themes, children explore diverse aspects of written language.

As an early childhood professional, you use your knowledge about children's typical discoveries and typical patterns of development to provide instruction that is "challenging but achievable" (IRA/NAEYC 1998). You recognize that children construct their own schemas internally, but that social experiences can greatly facilitate this construction.

5

Discovering Children's
Literacy Knowledge

Break not the rose; its fragrance and beauty are surely sufficient:
Resting contented with these, never a thorn shall you feel.

—John Hay

"**M**y mom said the work we do at school is too easy." Joanie was the youngest of a large family who had gone through our school. Her mother was involved in volunteer activities at the school and knew many of the parents and other teachers. I had just begun teaching first grade and didn't know exactly what she or Joanie might have meant by "too easy," but after thinking about it I had to admit to myself that many of the activities we had been doing were not always challenging for all of the children.

A typical whole-group activity for us was to generate a list of words—for example, *long O* words (*goat, bone*). If used in the right way, such a list can serve as an excellent spelling resource for a child who comes across a tricky word while writing, or for someone who is looking for words to support a piece of poetry or a limerick. However, after making the list of words with the children, I would ask them to use it to draw a picture, to write a story, or to write sentences "including at least three *long O* words." The major criterion for success was to use *long O* words and to spell them correctly. Rather than putting together a meaningful piece of writing, the children focused on getting *long O* words into the piece.

Joanie meanwhile had already begun to use *long O* without my prompting. It was in her first and last name, and she was beginning to read stories and to write, which meant that she would have explored *long O*, a fairly common sound in the English language. Instead of helping her to develop her knowledge, my activities were actually limiting what she might learn. Instead of writing freely and developing schemas for a variety of genres and many spellings, she was focusing on getting spellings right. She was bringing papers

82

home showing that she was practicing many things she could already do and that she wasn't taking many new risks; her work always looked perfect. If I had let her control more of her writing, she may not have spelled *long O* words conventionally, but she would have learned to sort out the system.

I was asking for convention because I didn't understand that children have to reconstruct written language for themselves before they can fully understand how it works. By controlling my children's exploration, I was limiting their ability to grow. I was "breaking the rose"—many roses—and as a consequence, I was also feeling the thorns. Joanie's words were certainly not a compliment, and to top it off, I had to read my children's stories: "I go. I like a goat. I like a toad. . . . Am I done, Mrs. Owocki? Mrs. Owocki! Mrs. Owocki! Can I be done?"

Although spending too much time working with isolated skills, the children in my classroom were also engaging in other, more developmentally appropriate literacy experiences. They were listening to and discussing stories. They were responding to literature through drawing, coloring, clay, painting, and writing. They were contributing to the making of class books, recording scientific observations, and playing board games that I had developed explicitly for them. They were reading stories together in the book corner, writing all over the chalkboard, performing poetry, and participating in dramatic retellings. And, I was teaching skills during these activities, too.

Unfortunately, these activities were less productive than they could have been. Our procedure was to get the "work" done first—the teacher-directed stuff and workbook exercises—and then we could get creative. You may have heard colleagues say that they balance instruction in phonics with developmentally appropriate practices because kids need both. This is what I was trying to do, not realizing that developmentally appropriate practices *are* balanced. Developmentally appropriate teachers *do* teach phonics. You help children to develop phonics knowledge every time you invite them to read, write, and share language in a social community. You are part of that community, and as a developmentally sensitive teacher, you constantly watch for ways to facilitate phonics knowledge in a meaningful way and constantly plan for phonics exploration. You model strategies for getting ideas on paper, for inventing spellings and for locating conventional spellings. You draw attention to letter-sound relationships, to rhymes, and to interesting words and language patterns. You model strategies for decoding text using multiple cueing systems. What you don't do is assume that all of the children in your classroom could benefit from the same kind of instruction, focusing on the same skill on the same day. What you don't do is separate skills instruction from real-life reading and writing. You know that learners construct knowledge and need to engage in learner-centered thinking to do so. You know that learners have diverse knowledge and diverse needs, and you teach based on what you know about your individual children.

Too many of my discussions with parents and too many of the papers I sent home reflected the "work" part of our day. I needed a way to track and understand the literacy accomplishments we were making through the developmentally appropriate activities. This would have shown me, the children, and their families the value of these activities in facilitating literacy development. Only when classrooms are set up for children and teachers together to explore literacy in meaningful, contextualized situations can we learn about children and teach based on their individual knowledge. Learning about children's knowledge is not easily done through preplanned, predetermined curriculum because it limits what they do naturally.

The message from Joanie was a painful thorn in my finger, but I can't say that I made immediate changes. Effective change requires time—for practice and reflection. My colleague Susie Emond says that sometimes we have to begin with baby steps to get where we're going; we have to clearly understand and have trust in what we are doing before we can make big changes in our teaching. Ten years after working with Joanie, I am still learning to let my students have more control over their learning. I think this is a typical struggle for teachers. We are always seeking a balance between letting students learn in a way that is natural and meaningful to them, and making sure that they develop the kinds of understandings we think are important. But isn't that what developmentally appropriate teaching is all about?

The developmentally appropriate teacher makes it a primary goal to discover children's literacy knowledge and learn about their strengths and interests. We turn next to some general information-seeking and observation strategies that you can use to inform the creation of a meaningful play environment. We then move on to explore a set of observation techniques to be used in evaluating children's uses of written language in play.

SEEKING AND SHARING INFORMATION

Children's ability to become personally engaged in play has a direct effect on how much they learn (Isenberg and Jalongo 1997). What do you need to know about your children to ensure that they can become personally engaged as they play in your classroom? As with any kind of teaching, you need to learn about children's individual interests and knowledge, and about their sociocultural contexts for living and growing (Bredekamp and Copple 1997).

Three ways to gain this information are by observing the play themes your children create spontaneously, inquiring into their play preferences, and collaborating with their families.

Observing Children's Play Themes

The children scurry in from their outdoor exploration time with rosy cheeks and a look of wild excitement in their eyes. They are ghouls, goblins, witches, and warlocks. They have been using the outdoor climber as a haunted house. Their teacher, Curt, follows them inside and rearranges the indoor climber so that it can be used as a haunted house. He then pulls a box of masks from the shelf; three of the children immediately put masks on their faces. Curt knocks at the door of the climber, calling "Trick or treat!" Todd opens the door to give him some "candy." Karla puts a black mask over her eyes, climbs on to the "roof" with a wand, and wickedly proclaims, "I'm the witch's daughter. I'm the witch's daughter... Curt, do you want to be a father witch?"

What kinds of play themes do *your* children create? What roles do they take on when they are playing with blocks, climbing on the bars at outdoor exploration time, or sitting atop the classroom loft? Curt has observed his children pursuing a haunted house theme for a few days now. On this day, he decides to alter their play setting and contribute play props that will help them to meaningfully carry their play forward. You can help children become engaged in school play by observing and supporting their spontaneous play interests. Children's play often takes its direction from the setting and the available props, so it makes sense to contribute props and materials that children see as useful.

When it comes to setting up for sociodrama, you might start a school year with a home-living center. You can learn a lot about children by observing them play in this center. Most children are familiar with the routines and materials of home living, and this familiarity helps them to participate in and learn through home-living play. "The comfort of familiar surroundings that contain known objects is important. Under these circumstances all people engage in more complex interactions and are eager to try new things" (Roskos 1995, 8). If pencils, pads of paper, food packages, magazines, storybooks, and newspapers are part of the props you include, you'll get to see right away what your children know about using written language in the real world. However, it is a good idea to limit the number of literacy props that you put into the play area at one time, otherwise the children may play with everything and "use them up" instead of using them for their intended functional purposes (Roskos 1995).

Make a point to notice and remember what children's play interests are. Every time you see a dramatic play theme emerging, jot down what it is and who is involved. You might even keep a notebook on a shelf or a sticky-notepad in your pocket—just to take notes on what you observe during children's play. For example, if you have a home-living center in your classroom, note where your children go with their babies when they leave this center. Do they ever go grocery shopping? Do they go driving? Do they go to the day-care center? Do they transform the home-living center into a new setting, such as a store or a day-care center? Do they ever read or write as they play? Would a grocery-store center work in your classroom? Could you set up some cars with maps, fix-it manuals, tools, and materials for writing directions and making road signs? Would a pretend day-care center work? Observing the play themes that children spontaneously develop provides you with possibilities for later centers.

Inquiring into Play Preferences

Asking children what they like to play also provides useful information for facilitating play. You might remember from Chapter 2 that Curt and Trish's children write plans for play. These plans help the teachers to gain insight into children's play interests and to contribute props and literacy materials that the children might find useful. If Curt and Trish notice over time that children have not had a chance to carry out a choice, they can determine whether the materials and settings are meeting their intended purposes.

Christine gives her first-grade children four choices for centers each day. The children mark their selections on their plans. Christine uses the plans to learn which centers the children are hesitant to use and to help them expand their center-time choices. For example, if there is a group of children who rarely choose the literacy-oriented play centers, Christine can plan to play in the center for a period of time and invite these children to play with her. She can then observe their activity to see whether they are familiar with the materials and comfortable taking on play roles, and she can model suggestions for extending the play. Collecting children's choices over time lends insight into their play interests and into what they are learning through play, and helps teachers provide appropriate instruction.

Collaborating with Families

Families are an important source of information about children's play and literacy experiences. Developmentally appropriate practice requires that teachers have knowledge about individual children and the various contexts of their lives. For younger children, it is especially necessary for teachers to seek out this knowledge through partnerships with families (Bredekamp and Copple 1997). Questionnaires, home-school journals, and collaborative meetings are three worthwhile ways to partner with families, and all are useful resources for organizing and planning play.

Questionnaires

Parent responses to questionnaires provide useful information about children's out-of-school experiences (including their literacy experiences), and about their personal interests. The questionnaire in Figure 5–1 seeks information about the places children have visited.

Many children have shopped at a grocery store, visited a physician's office, and traveled in a motor vehicle. They are likely to be familiar with the props and the various literacy materials used in those settings. Familiarity will help the children to readily incorporate them into their play. Not as many children will have stayed at a campsite, shopped at a hardware store, or visited an optometrist's office. Depending on where children live and what they have experienced, their understandings and ways of exploring materials vary. If a child has never shopped for clothing, the incorporation of a "clothing store" is not necessarily inappropriate, but may mean that you will need to walk through the entire experience with your children or at least model the process of choosing and purchasing a piece of clothing. Another option is to take on the role of matchmaker, deliberately pairing or grouping children for play (Van Hoorn et al. 1993). For clothing-store play, it might help to pair a child who knows about shopping for clothing with one who has not had this experience. A child who has experience in a given setting is likely to be familiar with its literacy and other materials and to take leadership in bringing these materials into the play.

It may be helpful to also inquire into kinds of literacy experiences children are involved in outside of school. Questionnaires can be designed specifically around the children's reading and writing experiences (Figure 5–2). If children do hobbies or crafts or are adept at storytelling, computer games, or at reading traffic and other signs, then they have valuable resources to contribute to play. If you decide to equip your block center with street signs and maps, but none of the children has experiences reading these kinds of print, then extra care will be needed to help children understand their functions.

If Erica is learning to sew, if Peter is learning to cook, if Justine's father is taking driving lessons, if Sam's mother is learning to fix a car, then it would be a great idea to provide opportunities for them to explore these experiences—including the literacy materials that are related to these experiences—through their play. They will have familiar understandings on which to build new knowledge. Carefully designed play centers have an element of familiarity so that children can build, or help one another build, from their places of knowing. Their materials and design reflect the themes children create by themselves through play as well as the experiences they have had outside of school.

PLACES YOUR CHILD KNOWS

Over the course of the year, we will be setting up a variety of imaginative play centers. To help plan meaningful centers, please place a check by the places your child has visited. We will try to design centers that are consistent with the experiences of the children. Place a star by the centers you feel your child would particularly enjoy. Thank you!

_____ Airport	_____ Kennels
_____ Automobile Repair/	_____ Laundromat
Service Shop	_____ Library
_____ Bakery	_____ Market (fruit/vegetable)
_____ Bank	_____ Movie Theater
_____ Barber Shop/Beauty Salon	_____ Museum
_____ Campsite	_____ Nursing Home
_____ Circus	_____ Pet Shop
_____ Construction Site	_____ Play/Musical/Concert
_____ Dance Studio	_____ Post Office
_____ Day-Care Center	_____ Print/Copy Shop
_____ Dentist's Office	_____ Restaurant
_____ Doctor's Office	_____ Sporting Events
_____ Eye Doctor's Office	_____ Store—Clothing/Shoes
_____ Flea Market/Swap Meet/	_____ Ice Cream Stand
Auction	_____ Store—Grocery/Foods
_____ Garage Sale/Yard Sale	_____ Store—Hardware
_____ Garden Shop/Florist	_____ Store—Music
_____ Gas Station	_____ Travel Agency
_____ Gym/Recreation Center	_____ Video Rental Shop
_____ Hospital	_____ Veterinarian
_____ Ice Cream Stand	_____ Zoo

Other Familiar Places: _____

_____

_____

Figure 5–1. Places Your Child Knows

READING AND WRITING AT HOME

We have been working at helping the children to bring reading and writing into their play. To plan this kind of instruction, it helps to know what the children are already doing at home. Please place a check by the kinds of reading and writing experiences your child engages in outside of school. Thank you!

_____ Reads or writes while playing (grocery list, menu)
_____ Plays games involving print (board games, matching games, cards)
_____ Does hobbies or crafts that involve written instructions
_____ Draws pictures
_____ Writes (scribbling, notes, letters, stories, names)
_____ Tells stories
_____ Says or listens to nursery rhymes or finger plays
_____ Reads, looks at, or listens to storybooks
_____ Looks at other books (cookbooks, magazines, newspapers)
_____ Plays computer games
_____ Cooks or bakes with you
_____ Watches television
_____ Writes lists (for shopping, to remember things)
_____ Reads print in the environment (traffic signs, store logos, cereal boxes, maps)
_____ Goes through mail, advertisements, catalogs
_____ Uses charts/calendar (chores, daily menu, weekly schedule)
_____ Sees you reading or writing. (Please give a few examples!)_____

Other reading/writing experiences: _____

Figure 5–2. Reading and Writing at Home

Informational Sessions

Informational sessions held early in the school year provide an especially good opportunity to get family members talking about what they do to facilitate literacy at home. A question such as "What kinds of things do you do to help your children learn to read and write?" might initially yield pat responses such as "I read to her." "I'm teaching him to write names." Write these ideas down on a large piece of chart paper, but don't let them stop there. It is important to construct idea lists *with* or *for* families that emphasize ideas other than storybook reading and writing (although these are certainly important). Family members may not be cognizant that their varied uses of written language have a great influence on children's literacy development (Auerbach 1995).

After you chart the family members' responses to your initial question, you might probe further ("Do you ever cook with your child?"), or ask them to generate more ideas in small groups. Once the flow of ideas starts, it can be hard to stop. Family members appreciate a list of ideas to carry out at home as well as tips for carrying them out. You can record and make copies of the information generated by the groups, or you can have a preestablished set of ideas prepared to pass out on the spot (see Figure 5–3).

NINE PLAYFUL WAYS TO HELP KIDS
LEARN TO READ AND WRITE

Read at least one book per day to your child.
Tips:

- Sit in a comfortable place with good lighting. Have a stuffed animal join you! Occasionally point to the words as you read. Invite your child to read with you. Talk with your child and ask questions before, during, and after reading. Good questions: What do you predict will happen next? What do the pictures tell us? Why did the character do this/feel this way? How was the problem solved? Remember when . . . ? (For example, Remember when we ate porridge/ saw a bear/ walked in the woods?)
- Tell your child which parts of the story you like. What is funny to you? What makes you sad? What surprises you?
- If your child becomes restless, it's okay to stop! Try another book at another time.

Listen to your child read.
Tips:

- If your child gets stuck on a word, suggest reading the rest of the sentence and then coming back to that word. Give prompts: What does it start with? What would make sense? What would sound right? Can the pictures help?
- If things aren't making sense for your child, the book may be too difficult or may not capture the child's interest.
- Making mistakes is a normal part of learning to read. If we try to help by

---

Figure 5–3. Nine Playful Ways to Help Kids Learn to Read and Write

correcting every mistake, children start to worry about how they sound rather than what they are reading.

- Suggest that your child read into a tape recorder, or to younger siblings.

Add reading writing materials to the child's play areas.
Tips:

- What does your child play often? Try to find, make, or have your child make reading and writing materials to enrich this play. For example, if your child likes miniature cars, make street signs, maps, billboards, or fix-it manuals. If your child likes to play with toy animals, pick up some library books on those animals (both fiction and informational) and include those in the play area.

Leave notes for your child, even if he/she can't read them yet.
Ideas:

- Leave notes in your child's lunchbox or school bag; leave them on the kitchen table, on the refrigerator, on the nightstand, or even in a shoe!
- Leave notes to say: Thank You; Good Morning; Good Night; Please pick up your room; I Love You; I Miss You; I'm sorry; Grandma's coming to visit; Have a wonderful day.

Provide a special place for writing and art activities.
Ideas:

- Suggest making character-props for retelling stories. Felt cutouts, popsicle-stick puppets, sock puppets, or paper cutouts work well.
- Suggest writing a note to/drawing a picture for a relative or friend. Mail it!
- Suggest drawing a picture and writing a label, a sentence, or a story to tell about it. Younger children often prefer to draw before, rather than after, writing.
- Collect old magazines, catalogs, and advertisements. Appealing pictures can be cut out and taped into a notebook. Pictures can be labeled, or stories written.
- Help your child collect familiar words from magazines, catalogs, or food packages. Children can often read street signs and logos from familiar foods and toys, and will enjoy showing their knowledge.

(continues)

Figure 5–3. (*continued*)

Cook and bake with your child.
Ideas:

- Browse cookbooks together and choose a recipe you both like. As you work, talk about the recipes and the print on the food packages.
- When you need a grocery list, make one together.
- Create recipes of your own and write them down. Here are two to play with:

  Yogurt Drinks—Blend together any combination of yogurt, juice, fruit, and crushed ice. Top with a choice of cinnamon, brown sugar, honey, or candy sprinkles.

  Trail Mix—Mix together any combination of pretzels, nuts, cereal, animal crackers, raisins, chewable candies, dried fruit, marshmallows, granola, caramel corn, miniature crackers, miniature cookies.

Notice and talk about the print all around you.
Ideas:

- Read traffic, street, and local business signs.
- Read place mats, menus, pamphlets, and posters.
- Read cereal boxes, toy packages, and hobby or game instructions.
- Browse through catalogs, magazines, and newspapers.
- Teach the letters of the alphabet through the print in the environment.
- Collect words your child can read in a notebook or on 3-by-5-inch notecards.

Share stories.
Tips:

- Listen to the stories your child tells.
- Help your child retell stories from books.
- Encourage your child to draw a picture to help tell a story.
- Help your child understand that stories often have a problem that is creatively solved.

(continues)

Figure 5–3. (*continued*)

Play language games.
Ideas:

- Say or read nursery rhymes together.
- Take turns making up lines for rhymes or sayings:
  Annie likes astronauts; Ben likes bugs.
  A more sophisticated form:
  Annie's ant eats apples; Ben's bear eats buns.
- These games can be turned into book-making projects. Write down the sayings over the course of a few days, and let the child illustrate.
- Play "I spy . . ." something that begins with the *ch* sound; something that starts like *popcorn;* something that rhymes with *moon.*

Figure 5–3. (*continued*)

Many family members want guidance on helping their children learn to read (Tracey 1995). Many do not understand what we mean when we tell them they must read to their children, or they may be unsure about how to help their child become interested in a book, how to talk to the child during the reading, what to do about the pictures, and what to do with the title (Edwards 1995). In turn, many teachers do not understand what parents do as they read with their children (Tracey 1995). It might be interesting to examine this practice at an informational session by asking parents "What do you do while reading with your child?" Although questions like this could be placed on a literacy questionnaire, it is likely that a little verbal probing would be helpful in getting in-depth response.

Over the course of the school year, informational sessions can be used to share progress and to talk about the kinds of things families have been doing with their children. Family members can be asked to bring in a book their child enjoys, a piece of writing their child has constructed at home, or a piece of environmental print for a group discussion on how literacy can be facilitated through everyday living.

Brainstorming reading and writing ideas with family members can lead you naturally to explain how play and other daily living experiences facilitate literacy in the classroom. It might be helpful to prepare a videotape, a slide show, a photo album (with enlarged pictures), or transparencies, so that your families can see their children in action at school. (Copy shops can make color transparencies directly from photographs.) For example, if you have a photograph of children playing in a store center, point out the cash register, the signs, the receipts, and the food packages, and explain to the families how these materials are used to help children develop their literacy knowledge. Tell what you do to support them as they use these materials, and discuss the ways in which peers help one another to learn. If you have a photograph of children writing together, discuss the ways in which talk and social problem solving help children to develop new understandings. I find it helpful to prepare a little list or a few notecards to guide my thinking during such talks.

Informational sessions are also a good time to invite families to contribute play props. Empty food containers, empty packages from around the house (seed packets, toy packages, cardboard containers) old magazines, newspapers, catalogs, and junk mail make wonderful play props and often reflect the language and/or cultural backgrounds of the children. If we want to encourage meaningful uses of literacy in naturally developing play themes, then the play environments must be reflective of the life and culture of the children (Neuman and Roskos 1992).

Remember, both you and the families with whom you work have important information to share. You have important information to share because you have professional knowledge that is interesting and useful to family members. Family members have information about their children's knowledge, interests, and experiences that is essential to effective teaching.

Home-School Journals

Home-school journals are another useful source of information for planning and learning about children, particularly if family members are unable to visit your classroom or attend conferences and informational sessions (or if they are for some reason hesitant about coming into the school). Journal pages are kept in a pocket folder or a three-ring binder. Some teachers use home-school journals to chat informally with families. They send short notes and messages back and forth, such as "Daniel held a chick today at school" "When we took Daniel to the state fair, he especially enjoyed petting the baby animals." The child may take part in this exchange: "I pet the animals at the state fair." Other teachers send a storybook or activity idea with the journal, asking that the child and parent write down what they thought of the story or comment on the activity. Other teachers use the journals to engage in dialogue with families about their children. The teacher initiates the dialogue with questions such as: What are some things your child likes to play at home? Does your child ever write at home? If so, what? Does your child ever draw or color at home? Does your child have a favorite book? A form (see Figure 5–4) can be prepared to facilitate communication. Once rapport begins to build, more in-depth dialogues can occur:

LET'S TALK ABOUT PLAY!

Child's Name: _____ Date: _____

During play today, your child:

Through this play, your child showed knowledge about:

Have you seen your child do anything similar at home?

Your child enjoys playing in the following play centers:

What does your child enjoy playing at home?

Figure 5–4. Let's Talk About Play!

Siobhan made a detailed set of animals out of play dough today. She used blocks for cages and made a sign to label each cage. She is still mostly playing by herself. When other children talk with her or try to share materials, she clutches them to herself or tries to take them to another part of the room. Have you noticed anything similar at home? I am working on a list of ideas—I'll send them home with Siobhan tomorrow. Do you have any ideas?

Vince has been engaging in some very imaginative super-hero play! This seems to be his favorite thing to do during play time. We are working on getting him to enjoy some of the play centers. Today he played at the rice table.

I teach a yearlong course on action-research in early childhood classrooms. This year, three of my students researched the initiation and use of home-school journals in their classrooms. They found that the journals were particularly beneficial in helping them (1) get to know children and their families; (2) become more sensitive and responsive to the children's lives outside of school (Adcock 1998); (3) understand the kinds of written language being used in the homes (Johnson 1998); and (4) gain insight into the children's literacy knowledge (King 1998).

KIDWATCHING LITERACY THROUGH PLAY

Play is a useful medium for gathering information about children's literacy knowledge because it frees children to show their real-world abilities. We assess children to improve classroom practice, and to inform the educational decisions we make about them (Bredekamp and Copple 1997; Isenberg and Jalongo 1997). The information gained in assessing literacy through play can be used to inform all kinds of instruction, not only that which occurs during play.

Three common methods for gathering information about children's literacy are observation and anecdotal note taking, collecting written language samples, and informal questioning. These tools are used to chart and track children's development with the goal of providing an explicit picture of what children know about written language. As you use these tools, the following questions may help you to organize your thinking:

- What knowledge about written language do my children show as they play?
- What do their unconventional uses of written language reveal about their knowledge?
- How can my observations inform my teaching?

These are *kidwatching* questions (Goodman 1978). *Kidwatching* is recording and reflecting on the knowledge that children demonstrate in a variety of social and cultural settings. Teachers who kidwatch recognize signs of development and know what children's unconventional uses of written language indicate about their thinking. They use this information to guide their curriculum and teaching.

How Kidwatching Works

The following interaction between Karen and her four-year-old student, Erin, provides a model for kidwatching literacy through play in your own classroom and for using anecdotal records, written language samples, and informal questioning as part of your assessment.

Erin writes E-R-I-H-H-D, and then moves her pencil across the letters several times, moving her lips as if she is reading.

Erin: Karen, I wrote *bottle.* Karen, I wrote *bottle.*

Karen: You wrote what?

Erin: Bottle.

Karen: [*looking at Erin's paper.*] *Bottle?* Wow, look at that, Erin. You wrote *bottle.*

Erin continues to write more words and to read back what she has written. Later, she looks for the page where she had written bottle.

Erin: [*softly to herself*] Where's *bottle?* Where's *bottle?* [*She finds where she had written E-R-I-H-H-D.*] See? *Bottle.* Two-two-one-one-one-one." [*while pointing to the letters E-R-I-H-H-D*]

What knowledge about written language does Erin show as she plays? What do her unconventional uses of written language reveal about her knowledge? First, Erin has conventional control over many letter forms. She uses letters from her own pool of language information (many from her own name) to construct the spelling of several words. Second, she shows her understanding that symbols carry meaning. The letters she puts together mean something to her, and she even goes back to read them later, showing her understanding that once something has been written, its meaning does not change. Third, Erin shows a sense of directionality. Her writing of *bottle,* and of all of the other words she wrote in this example, proceeded from left to right and top to bottom. Fourth, Erin shows a developing sense of what a word is. Her word E-R-I-H-H-D is the same length as the word *bottle* and is part of a list of words that are all separated by spaces. Erin did not choose to use a page full of letters to represent bottle; she wrote one short string of letters that actually looks like a word. Finally, Erin is confident about inventing spellings for the words she wants to write.

The next step is to ask How do Karen's observations inform her teaching? What can she do based on her observation of Erin's writing? First, she needs to collect a variety of information so that she can carefully and systematically learn about Erin's knowledge. Writing samples, anecdotal records, and informal questioning can help her.

Gathering Information

Contained within Erin's journal is a *writing sample,* a piece of written language that has been produced in a meaningful context. As a kidwatcher, Karen might choose to make a copy of the sample or jot an *anecdotal note* to herself to remember the event. An anecdotal note is a brief written account of an event worth remembering; it provides a description of the event, and may or may not include a quotation or a sample of oral language. She will also record the date of the event. Depending on time, Karen could record something as simple as *Erin—writing in journal: E-R-I-H-H-D = bottle,* or if she writes what happened at a later time, she might write something as elaborate as *Erin—writing in journal: Smiling and pointing to her journal page. Said, "Karen, I wrote bottle! I wrote bottle!" (E-R-I-H-H-D = bottle.) I asked a few times, because I don't remember seeing her do this kind of thing in her journal before. She even seems to have written other words, too. Need to look back in journal to see if she's been doing similar word-length lists. We could pick up on this. What kinds of lists could we construct together to support her understandings?* The elaborated note includes what Karen observed during the event as well as the information she gained from her *informal question. Informal questions* (as a medium for collecting information about children's literacy knowledge) are aimed at learning about what the child was thinking as the literacy event was occurring (Vukelich 1995).

Once Karen has collected information on Erin (preferably from several literacy events), she must reflect on all that she has seen. It is helpful to keep all of the information collected on children in one place. Hanging file folders provide easy access to materials, and are compact for storing. Every time you gather a new piece of information, you just place it in the child's file folder. (If you use portfolios for assessment, this information can be kept in the portfolio.) When you go to reflect and plan, all of your information is in one place.

Analyzing and Reflecting

Information gathering is not of much use in informing educational decision making unless we use our professional knowledge to reflect on what we observe. Karen, after collecting several samples of writing and several anecdotal records from Erin, can pull out Erin's file folder and use it to think about what the child knows, and what this might mean for instructing her (the *kidwatching* questions). This process can be facilitated by creating a literacy checklist—a set of competencies your children may demonstrate during play.

Using a Checklist

Checklists can be helpful for analyzing the information you have gathered while observing play. The Early Literacy Checklist for Play (Figure 5–5) contains literacy elements that can easily be observed as preschool, kindergarten, or first-grade children are playing. Like any checklist, you need to adapt it to match the goals you have for the children in your classroom. Checklists do not replace collecting anecdotal records and writing samples, but they can be useful in putting together a meaningful picture of what children are learning through play.

When you are ready for some in-depth reflection, pull out your file folders on a few children and use your checklist to consider what they know about written language. Although we have only seen one example from Erin, we can note on the checklist that she spends time writing, she understands that written symbols carry meaning, she attempts to make oral language match the graphic characteristics of text, she writes using random strings of alphabet letters, and

---

LITERACY CHECKLIST FOR PLAY

During play time at school, _____ has been observed:

Acting as a literate member of the community.
_____ reads to support play themes
_____ writes to support play themes
_____ spends time looking at books/other reading material
_____ spends time writing/using the writing center
_____ shares reading/writing ideas with friends
_____ accepts reading/writing ideas from friends
_____ actively problem solves (seeks out spellings, meanings of words)

Discovering stories and story language.
_____ plays out pretend story lines
_____ creates drawings, paintings, or sculptures that tell a story
_____ uses puppets, masks, or props to dramatically retell a story
_____ dramatic retellings include _____ characters, _____ setting,
_____ conflict, _____ plot episodes, _____ resolution
_____ dramatic retellings include story language (once upon a time, the next
day, the end)
_____ dramatic retellings demonstrate critical insights

Exploring the features and forms of written language.
_____ shows understanding that written symbols carry meaning
_____ makes predictions about text
_____ attempts to make oral language match with parts of written text
_____ copies letters or words
_____ writes using invented cursive or letterlike forms
_____ writes using random strings of alphabet letters

(continues)

Figure 5–5. Literacy Checklist for Play

_____ purposefully manipulates random strings of letters to make them say different things

_____ breaks words into syllables (orally or in writing)

_____ writes using initial consonants

_____ writes using initial and final consonants

_____ writes using initial and final consonants and vowels (some conventional spellings)

_____ writes using many conventional spellings

_____ writes left-to-right, top-to-bottom

_____ puts spaces between words

_____ experiments with punctuation

Exploring books and book language.

_____ holds book right-side-up

_____ turns pages left-to-right

_____ labels or makes up sentences about pictures in a book

_____ pretends to read while turning through pages of a book

_____ reads books with familiar patterns or repetitive language

_____ pays attention to some of the print while reading

_____ reads the print (errors are to be expected)

Exploring the many ways in which written language is used in our worlds.

_____ announcements/ reports	_____ diaries/journals	_____ menus
_____ advertisements	_____ eye charts	_____ music and songs
_____ bills	_____ fiction (storybooks)	_____ newspapers
_____ blueprints	_____ food and other packages	_____ notes and letters
_____ book reviews		_____ pamphlets
_____ calendars/ schedules	_____ forms	_____ plans
	_____ graphs	_____ poetry
_____ cash registers/ money	_____ greeting cards	_____ posters
	_____ instructions	_____ prescriptions
_____ charts	_____ invitations	_____ programs
_____ checks	_____ labels	_____ price tags
_____ clocks	_____ lists	_____ receipts
_____ comics	_____ library cards	_____ recipes
_____ computers	_____ magazines	_____ signs
_____ coupons	_____ maps	_____ tickets
_____ diagrams	_____ manuals	_____ weather reports

(*continues*)

Figure 5–5. (*continued*)

Other _____

_____

Summary Statement of Knowledge Demonstrated:

Ideas for Instruction:

Figure 5–5. (*continued*)

she explores the function of a journal. With only one example, it is not possible to reflect on the instruction she might need, but based on what we know, we can encourage her to continue her writing and watch for how she sorts out her ideas about the conditions that make a piece of writing interpretable. It might also be a good idea to find other ways for her to explore lists, since this is what she seems to be doing in this event.

Play checklists help to analyze data and put it into interpretable form, but they cannot provide the rich details or the broad perspective that anecdotal records combined with writing samples can provide. Used together, these sources of information can paint a comprehensive picture of what children know about written language. By collecting information over the course of a school year, you can gain substantial insight into children's expected next steps and provide valuable opportunities for them to explore those steps.

CONCLUSION

Recognizing the beginnings of written language development equips adults to assist children as they explore and hone their literacy learning (Goodman 1996) and enables them to anticipate where children might go next in their literacy-related thinking. Effective teaching is based on what we expect children to be doing tomorrow. To teach toward children's tomorrows requires that we understand today how they become readers and writers, and that we customize that understanding to fit each child. Only then can we help them attain their highest potential as readers and writers.

6

Developing the Literate Play Environment

Leslie and Athena, first graders in Christine Eaton's classroom, are making a sign for the class store:

Athena: How about if we call it The Sending Store, because there are stamps?

Leslie: [*looking over the items in the store*] Hmm . . . how about The Food Store?

Christine: [*pointing to some of the other items in the store*] How about the food *and* something else store?

Leslie: And . . . and . . . and . . . toy!

Leslie writes, the food and toy store, *and then tapes the sign to the wall.*

Taking an active role in developing play centers gives children a sense of ownership over the play environment. As Leslie and Athena help with setting up the store center, they contribute materials and ideas from their own perspectives, making the center a place that is meaningful to them. The teacher contributes materials and ideas from the adult perspective, helping the children to expand their thinking and develop new understandings. The design of the play environment is extremely important because it influences how engaged children will become and how constructively they will use the available materials.

TIPS FOR DESIGNING LITERACY-RELATED PLAY CENTERS

1. *Establish a literacy-rich play atmosphere.* Your children will become most involved in reading and writing if you can create with them a literacy-rich play atmosphere. A literacy-rich play atmosphere is one in which you and your children use written language, as it is

needed, *to serve real-life functions* in play. Unless children see that reading and writing serve a function in play, they will have very little reason to use them. As you teach through play centers, your role is to support and extend their spontaneous uses of written language and to model and demonstrate as many meaningful uses as you can. (See Chapter 4 for a description of the functions of written language.)

2. *Establish a print-rich play environment.* Children are most likely to read and write in an environment containing many familiar, useful reading and writing materials. Make sure the children have access to these materials during play. A typical print-rich play environment includes many shapes and sizes of paper, empty booklets, notepads, pencils, crayons, and markers. All kinds of books are accessible. Thematic centers include all of the types of print that would be found in, for example, a post office, a veterinary office, a hair salon, or a fast-food restaurant. Children in a print-rich play environment are not expected to automatically use written language without support, although they often do. As a facilitator of literacy through play, you are on watch to model, make suggestions, and capitalize on children's teachable moments.

3. *Provide literacy materials that foster open-ended exploration.* Open-ended exploration allows children to be creative and to use materials in a way that is meaningful to them. A blank piece of paper and a box of markers offer several open-ended possibilities for exploration. Children can use them to support their play in a variety of ways. Open-ended materials help children to explore and build on what they know.

4. *Provide literacy materials that constrain exploration.* What? Constrain children's exploration? Yes! Materials that offer fewer possibilities for exploration constrain children's thinking, or direct their attention toward certain conventions. A medical record and a pencil suggest fewer possibilities than a blank piece of paper and box of markers, but they are as important as the open-ended materials. With a medical record, children fill in blanks and check boxes on a form that is designed for a specific purpose. By interacting with conventional materials, children make discoveries about the real-life conventional features of written language.

5. *Introduce literacy props to familiar play areas* (Roskos 1995). If children play in settings similar to those they have experienced

in real life, they may already have a good idea of how to use the literacy props in those settings. For example, children familiar with grocery shopping may have ideas about using grocery lists, coupons, and advertisements. They can build new knowledge from a place of knowing. If you set up a veterinary office, but few of your children have experience in that setting, then the literacy exploration may not be as meaningful. Observing children's naturally occurring play themes, writing back and forth in journals with parents, and making use of questionnaires (see Chapter 5) can provide you with play contexts and literacy experiences that your children find familiar.

6. *Systematically collect literacy materials.* Start a collection of literacy materials to be used in dramatic play centers. To enrich your home-living center, think of all the literacy materials that might be found in your children's homes and start collecting! When putting together a collection of literacy items for a play center, make a visit to the real-life setting. Go to the dentist's office or the hair salon, and ask for literacy materials. At first, people often think that they don't have anything appropriate for children, but once they get the hang of it, they find all kinds of materials to donate.

7. *Store literacy materials for dramatic play in an accessible location.* Easy-to-find materials expedite the process of setting up play centers. More important, when you find spontaneous moments in play to introduce or model a use of written language, you have the necessary materials at your fingertips. I store workplace literacy materials in large envelopes, so that I can simply pull them off the shelf when I need them.

8. *Avoid clutter.* If you provide too many materials at once (including too many literacy materials), the children may not use them constructively. Children may "use them up" instead of exploring their possibilities (Roskos 1995). Select a few literacy materials at a time, and help your children understand how to use them in meaningful ways. If they are not using materials appropriately, or if they find it difficult to pick up and organize materials when play time is over, think about whether the center is overloaded with materials.

9. *Establish boundaries between play areas.* What do children do when you take them to the gym, the playground, or to a big, open space? They run! Large amounts of empty space entice children to run, chase, and engage in large-motor play. Smaller spaces invite them

to engage in dramatic and constructive play (Johnson, Christie, and Yawkey 1987) and to talk and play quietly (Roskos 1995). Boundaries are typically established by placing tables, shelves, storage bins, or other furniture between play areas. Putting boundaries between play areas does not mean that children cannot carry materials back and forth. In fact, interesting things can happen when a cash register and some play money is brought into the block area or when dolls are brought to the book corner.

10. *Purposefully plan traffic patterns.* Direct traffic away from areas that require privacy, intense concentration, electrical cords, or open containers of water. Avoid sending heavy traffic through areas in which block structures may be knocked down or painters' elbows may be bumped. Place centers in which water is needed (art, science, water tables) near a water source (Brewer 1992). Art centers need a trash can.

11. *Establish quiet zones.* Quiet zones allow children to concentrate and collaborate. Quiet zones are not without talk, but they provide an atmosphere for the kind of thinking, discussion, and listening that would be required while playing with puppets, while reading, or while writing. Place all of your quiet centers in the same part of the classroom (Brewer 1992) to create a quiet zone. Noisier play spaces, such as woodworking and aerobic exercise areas should have their own area of the classroom.

12. *Establish private zones.* Children may appreciate the opportunity to spend some peaceful time by themselves during the day. Crowded conditions, interacting continuously, and frequent interruptions can cause fatigue and frustration (Kostelnik et al. 1993), which inevitably lead to conflicts. Private zones provide a relaxing retreat for children, and allow them, if they desire, to view others without necessarily interacting with them (Lowman and Ruhmann 1998). My friend Della provides a private zone by devoting a corner of her classroom to an old bathtub full of pillows; my mother had a couch walled off by wooden bookshelves; my friend Kathy has a loft with a private "upper room." In my classroom, I had an upright refrigerator box with an arched doorway.

13. *Include soft areas in your classroom.* Soft areas are comfortable and relaxing to children (Kostelnik et al. 1993). Soft areas are made with pillows, cushions, colors, curves (Brewer 1992), and malleable play materials such as play dough, sand, and water (Kostelnik

et al. 1993). (There is nothing wrong with hard materials such as blocks, hard floors, and wooden chairs, but we want to make sure that part of the atmosphere conveys warmth.)

14. *Think about how you will watch over all of the centers.* You can only be in one place at one time. Does more than one center require careful supervision? If so, parents are often glad to help. Another option (if you are the only adult present and need to carefully watch over one center in particular) is simply to ensure that all of the other centers can be self-started by the children, and that they will require minimal participation on your part.

15. *Continually self-evaluate your role in facilitating literacy through play.* The self-evaluating teacher asks:

    • Do my children read and write during play? Are the materials meaningful?

    • Do I take time to capitalize on teachable moments?

    • What functions does literacy serve in my children's play? Are my children exploring a variety of genres and forms of written language? Do they have the materials they need for feature exploration?

    Our actions in the classroom are guided by our beliefs about the ways in which children think and learn. When we are conscious of these beliefs, and when we reflect on our actions, these entities come into alignment (Pierce 1993).

An awareness of the influence that the physical environment has on children's actions and behaviors is good motivation to carefully consider its design. When centers do not run smoothly, or children do not become engaged in play, always ask yourself whether something in the physical environment may be the cause. The environment is easy to manipulate, and worth manipulating because it has such a strong effect on what children do and how they behave. The following section looks at a set of ideas for designing and facilitating literacy through twelve specific play centers.

TWELVE PLAY CENTERS

The descriptions in this section provide ideas for conceptualizing and developing your own play centers, and for tailoring them to the interests, experiences, and needs of your children. Each description contains ideas for helping children to *build schemas* to support their play, for stocking the center with *materials,* for organizing the *setting,* for suggesting play *roles and viewpoints,* and for *scheduling.* The ideas are compatible for preschool, kindergarten, and first-grade classrooms. Of course, the way you use the ideas will depend on your grade level, your classroom, and your children's interests and experiences. The following centers are included:

- Author and Illustrator's Studio
- Construction Site
- Grocery Store
- Home-Living Center
- Library
- Newsroom
- Pet Store
- Post Office
- Restaurant
- School
- Science Laboratory
- Weather Station

As you design play centers, you may have one thing in mind for your children, but find that they use the materials in a completely unexpected way. Go ahead and take their lead as you teach. By allowing them to maintain control of the play, they will build new knowledge in a way that makes sense to them. If you are hoping for your children to explore a particular concept through a center, plan to spend more time there, observing, suggesting, and modeling specific behaviors and actions as necessary. If you teach older children, you may demonstrate possibilities for using the centers before children actually play in them. (Chapter 2 shows in detail how a preschool and a first-grade teacher help children to learn specific concepts through play.)

The roles and viewpoints sections are designed to give you ideas for extending play and for connecting it with content-area themes. I have suggested only a few ideas to help you get your thinking started, but the possibilities are endless. Roles and viewpoints may be modeled, suggested, and discussed before, during, and after play. All of the ideas contained in the following sections are for picking and choosing, based on your children's interests, needs, and experiences.

Author and Illustrator's Studio
SCHEMA BUILDING:

- As you read with children, discuss the role of the author and illustrator.
- Read biographies and autobiographies of children's authors and illustrators.

- Create class books with your children, modeling use of the studio materials.

MATERIALS:

- variety of shapes, sizes, and colors of paper
- markers, crayons, pencils, and pens
- scissors, tape, stapler
- books to use as references
- folder for each child to store work-in-progress
- list of words that your children use often

Note: A preschool list of words (always created *with* the children) contains the names of the children in the class, the names of the teachers, and other commonly used words such as *mom, dad, I love you, dog, cat, to, dear,* and *from.* With older children, you can construct a more extensive list of words, focusing on those that they use most often in their writing.

SETTING:

- In a well-lighted quiet zone, set up a table with a shelf right next to it. Place an easel nearby. The bookshelf holds all of the materials listed above, and is neatly organized. The easel may be used for illustrating.
- To achieve softness, bring in an old lamp, make cushions for the chairs, and place this center near a window.

ROLES AND VIEWPOINTS:

- What kinds of books can authors write? (Discuss genre possibilities.) What do illustrators do? How are illustrations in storybooks different from illustrations in nonfiction books? Do authors and illustrators only create books? What else do they create? (magazines, pamphlets, brochures, manuals).
- Consider connecting the author and illustrator center to class inquiry themes. For example, if your class is investigating homes the children could write and illustrate fiction and nonfiction books having something to do with homes (including animal homes).

SCHEDULING:

- Children may spontaneously engage in author and illustrator play.
- Children may be scheduled to work in the center each day or on a weekly basis.

Construction Site

SCHEMA BUILDING:

- View a home-building video.
- Invite a builder, construction worker, or architect to the classroom to give a 5–10 minute talk and to show some occupational materials. (Prepare interview questions in advance.)
- Tour a home-improvement retail store.

MATERIALS:

- blocks (Try different sizes and shapes.)
- hardhats and goggles
- buckets and paintbrushes
- tool kit
- workbench (a table or empty crate)
- blueprints and plans
- plastic connecting pipes, coiled plastic (for wiring), brooms for cleaning up
- builders' reference books and trade magazines
- open-ended literacy materials for making blueprints, plans, and signs (Caution, Road Crew, STOP)

SETTING:

- Provide a workbench and open floor space on a low-pile rug. (Rugs will reduce the noise level in the area.)
- Place blocks, tools, and other props on low shelves, next to the building area.

ROLES AND VIEWPOINTS:

- What does a construction worker do? An architect? A plumber? An electrician? A road builder? An excavator?
- What tools (including literacy materials) do these workers need to accomplish their crafts?
- Consider connecting the construction center with class inquiry themes. For example, if you are studying homes, invite the children to draw blueprints and home plans, or, if you are studying community workers, talk about which community workers build things.

SCHEDULING:

- Children may spontaneously engage in construction play.
- Provide large appliance boxes for scheduled teams of children to paint, floor, side, plumb, wire, and roof.

Grocery Store

SCHEMA BUILDING:

- Tour a grocery store to learn about the jobs of its various employees.
- Discuss the different jobs at a grocery store.
- Invite your children to bring in and talk about food packages.

MATERIALS:

- shelving (bookshelves, cardboard boxes, furniture from home-living area)
- checkout counter with pretend scanner, cash register, grocery bags
- shopping carts and baskets
- writing materials
- food packages and play foods
- newspaper advertisements, coupons
- aprons, rolling pins, measuring cups, and play dough for bakery
- money, checkbooks, credit cards, paper for receipts

SETTING:

- With help from children, shelve food by groups (Produce, Dairy, Bakery).
- Place a checkout counter at the store's exit area.
- Invite children to make signs (Farmer Jack, SALE, Bakery) and price tags.
- Invite children to make food packages or cut food pictures from magazines.
- Set up a table so that bakery workers will have a counter to work behind.
- Provide a recycling bin for shoppers to return food packages. (Provide another box to return foods that are not sold in packages). A shelf stocker can restock the shelves as food packages and foods are returned.

ROLES AND VIEWPOINTS:

- What does a cashier do? What is the role of a store manager? A shopper? A pharmacist? A baker? A butcher? A deli worker? A shelf stocker? How does the work of a farmer relate to what happens in a store? A truck driver?

- What tools (including literacy materials) do these workers need to accomplish their jobs?
- Consider connecting the grocery store center to class inquiry themes. For example, if your class is studying foods, you might emphasize choosing foods from the food pyramid, choosing nutritious foods, or playing out the farm-to-store progression.

SCHEDULING:

- Children may spontaneously engage in grocery store play.
- Older children: *Week One*—Design and set up a store with your children. *Week Two*—Schedule interested children to play in the store in groups. Children can choose the roles they would like to try.

Home-Living Center

SCHEMA BUILDING:

- Children will already have a good idea of what they can do with this center.
- As new literacy materials are introduced, watch how the children use them and model and make suggestions when teachable moments arise.

MATERIALS:

- men's and women's dress-up clothing, full-length mirror
- dress-up clothing for a variety of professions
- child-size furniture
- dolls (representing facial and skin features of different ethnic groups) and doll clothes
- foods, food packages, and dishes
- literacy materials that are representative of the materials found in children's homes (coupons, catalogs, newspapers, books, a message board, pens, pencils, markers, and paper)
- hooks and shelves for organizing and storing materials
- mops, brooms, dustpans, sponges, and rags
- stuffed animals (for pets)

SETTING:

- Organize small furniture into a semienclosed room (leave two wide entry/exit spaces).

- Furniture possibilities include toy sinks, stoves, refrigerators, and beds. Small tables, couches, and chairs are typically included. Invite the children to organize the materials from the above list just like they might be organized in a home.
- If possible, divide the center into a kitchen area and a living room area.

ROLES AND VIEWPOINTS:

- Who are the members of a family?
- What literacy materials do family members use as they go about their daily lives?

SCHEDULING:

- Children may spontaneously engage in home-living play.

Library

SCHEMA BUILDING:

- Visit a public library.
- Invite a librarian to the classroom to give a 5–10 minute talk and to show some occupational materials. (Prepare interview questions in advance.)
- Visit the school library. Each child checks out a book.

MATERIALS:

- table with chairs; small bookshelf with books to be checked out
- checkout counter with pretend scanner, keyboard, and telephone
- drop-box (cardboard box with a slit cut big enough to drop off books)
- two boxes for notecards (one labeled IN, one labeled OUT)
- notecards labeled with each book's author, illustrator, and title
- materials for writing

SETTING:

- Place the books near a table with chairs. Try to include at least twice as many books as there are children in your classroom. Place a checkout counter nearby. (To check out a book, a child signs his or her name on a card and moves it from the IN box to the OUT box. When books are returned, the cards are moved again.)
- The bookshelf is used to store only those books which may be checked out from the class library. Place a drop-box near the checkout counter.

- Decide whether checked-out books will be kept at school or taken home. Also, decide the length of the checkout period.

ROLES AND VIEWPOINTS:

- What does a librarian do? What does a shelf stocker do? What does a library patron do?
- What tools (including literacy materials) do these workers need to accomplish their jobs?
- Consider connecting the library center to class inquiry themes. For, example, if you are studying water, all of the books in the library could focus in some way on that theme.

SCHEDULING:

- Children may spontaneously engage in library play.
- One day per week can be set up for library play/checking out library books. Each child is asked to visit the library during center or play time on a particular day. Children may check out their own materials if no "librarian" is present. Younger children and children who are inexperienced at this process will need assistance.

Newsroom

SCHEMA BUILDING:

- Browse a local newspaper with your children, discussing items of interest and pointing out different genres.
- Model journalistic observation, interviewing, and note taking. You can do this modeling during children's play (Davidson 1995).
- Model writing in the various genres used in a newspaper.
- Invite a news professional to your classroom to give a 5–10 minute talk and to show some occupational materials. (Prepare questions in advance.)

MATERIALS:

- pens, pencils, markers, crayons, paper
- clipboards for taking notes
- large newsprint (or white paper) for publishing a newspaper
- old keyboards, old cameras, and a real computer if possible
- books and newspapers to use as reference material

SETTING:

- Designate a large table with nearby shelves (stocked with the items listed above) to function as the newsroom.
- Invite your children to make signs, badges, and press cards to identify their roles.

ROLES AND VIEWPOINTS:

- What are the different jobs in a newsroom? What does a reporter do? A journalist? An editor? A newspaper delivery person?
- What tools (including literacy materials) do these workers need to accomplish their jobs?
- Children may venture around the classroom making observations, taking notes, and conducting interviews, and then return to the newsroom to write. Others may remain in the newsroom, writing and organizing information.
- If you work with older children, you might tie the newsroom center to class inquiry themes. For example, if your class is studying friendship, you could invite your children to focus on this theme as they write news articles, drawings, advertisements, cartoons, and other items.

SCHEDULING:

- Children may spontaneously engage in newsroom play.
- A weekly or monthly paper can be prepared. Time is set aside on regular basis for all of the children to engage in newsroom play. Children can choose and try out a variety of roles.

Pet Store

SCHEMA BUILDING:

- Visit a pet store.
- Read children's literature on pets and pet care.
- Invite a pet-store worker to visit your classroom to give a 5–10 minute talk and show some occupational materials. (Prepare interview questions in advance.)

MATERIALS:

- pet books, magazines, and pet-care pamphlets
- pet posters

- cages (cardboard boxes) and beds (old rags)
- writing material to make price tags and labels for cages
- grooming materials, dishes, food (smallish round objects, or laminated pictures of pet food)
- schedule for watering, feeding, cleaning cages, exercise/walking, attention/love, and grooming (children place their initials or write their names by the jobs they have accomplished)
- stuffed animals, puppets, and/or miniature toy animals
- pet costumes
- cash register and money
- small broom, scrub-brush, rags, and bucket for cleaning cages

SETTING:

- Stack same-sized cardboard boxes to be used for cat and dog cages. Bird cages, terrariums, and aquariums can be used to house other pets such as birds and fish.
- Set up a table with a cash register, and various pet-related items to sell. For example, the children could sell dishes, empty pet-food containers, books on pets, and pet beds.

ROLES AND VIEWPOINTS:

- What do pet-store workers do? How do workers take care of the animals?
- What materials (including literacy materials) do they need to accomplish their jobs?
- What do pets-for-sale do? How might it feel to be in a cage for long periods of time?
- Where do pet-store animals come from? Are they sometimes endangered species?

SCHEDULING:

- Children may spontaneously engage in pet-store play.

Post Office
SCHEMA BUILDING:

- Browse with your children through a variety of letters and notes.
- Model letter writing and addressing envelopes.
- Tour a post office.

- Invite a post office worker to your classroom to give a 5–10 minute talk and to show some occupational materials. (Prepare interview questions in advance.)

MATERIALS:

- writing utensils, paper, greeting cards, envelopes, address books
- scale, stamps, stamp pads
- cash register, money
- packing forms, boxes, packaging material, tape
- mail bag, mail hat, class mailbox, individual mailboxes

SETTING:

- Set up a table for postal workers. Neatly organize the post office materials on a nearby shelf or on the table.
- Place a mailbox at the post office as well as in another part of the room. Each child in the class needs an individual mailbox. Cubbies, lockers, or shoe boxes can be used.

ROLES AND VIEWPOINTS:

- Who helps mail get delivered? What does a mail delivery person do? What does a post office worker do? What do pilots and truck drivers contribute?
- What tools (including literacy materials) do these workers use to accomplish their jobs?
- What conventions of written language do letter writers typically use?
- Tie post office play to class inquiry themes. For example, if you are studying rainforest animals invite your children to send for information from the World Wildlife Fund, the International Council for Bird Preservation, or the Earth Island Institute.
- If you are studying money, emphasize paying for stamps and packaging materials.

SCHEDULING:

- Children may spontaneously engage in post office play.
- Each child can be asked to send at least one note or letter through the post office.

Restaurant

SCHEMA BUILDING:

- Provide opportunities to browse through menus and restaurant advertisements.
- Tour a restaurant.
- Invite a restaurant worker to your classroom to give a 5–10 minute talk and show occupational materials. (Prepare interview questions in advance.)

MATERIALS

- menus, material for making menus
- order pads and pencils
- order sheets with foods already listed; waiter checks off desired items
- cookbooks and recipe cards
- chalkboards and chalk (for writing specials, prices, soup of the day)
- materials for making place mats, restaurant signs, and name tags for waiters
- play foods, food packages, and cooking utensils
- carry-out containers, dishes, napkins, and trays
- cash register, calculator, money, credit cards, checkbooks, receipts
- aprons and chef hats

SETTING:

- Set up a table and chairs for diners and a kitchen area for food preparation. Help children to select materials from the above list.
- Children can construct menus, place mats, recipes.

ROLES AND VIEWPOINTS:

- What does a waiter do? How about a cashier? A chef? A menu designer? An advertiser? A customer? A health inspector?
- What tools (including literacy materials) do these people need to carry out their duties?
- Older children: Tie restaurant play to class inquiry themes. For example, if you are investigating foods, you could invite the children to make menus (using drawing or writing) that include at least one item from each part of

the food pyramid. If you are investigating money, you could emphasize prices of foods, tabulating bills, and paying the cashier.

SCHEDULING:

- Children may spontaneously engage in restaurant play.
- Older children: *Week One*—Set up a work center to design menus, place mats, signs, and name tags. *Week Two*—Schedule interested children to play in the restaurant in groups. Children can choose the roles they would like to try.

Schoolroom

SCHEMA BUILDING:

- This may sound peculiar, but your children might enjoy playing in a miniature version of a classroom. You probably won't need to think much about helping the children to build background knowledge for this center. However, many children do play as students who are *older* than themselves. You might talk with the children about what their older siblings and friends do at school.

MATERIALS:

- chalkboard and chalk
- all kinds of books
- variety of other reading materials
- variety of paper and writing utensils
- an assortment of toys (for play time)
- materials for taking attendance, planning schedules, and writing notes to families

SETTING:

- Provide a small table and chairs (or desks) for the students. Provide a shelf or desk organizer for reading and writing materials.
- Place a special stool in the center for the teacher to read to the children. The teacher should also have a special shelf to store supplies.

ROLES AND VIEWPOINTS:

- What does a teacher do? What do students do? What is the role of a principal? A custodian? A lunchroom worker? A parent?

- What tools (including literacy materials) do these people need to accomplish their jobs?
- You may invite the children to focus their school play on a particular theme the class may be investigating. For example, if your class is investigating ways of keeping the environment clean, the books and toys included in the center could be related to that theme. Ask the "teacher" to help her "students" to read, write, and talk about environmental issues.

SCHEDULING:

- Children may spontaneously engage in schoolroom play.

Science Laboratory

SCHEMA BUILDING:

- Invite a biologist, geologist, chemist, archeologist, or ecologist to your classroom. (Prepare interview questions in advance.)
- Discuss hypothesis testing and recording written observations.

MATERIALS:

- white coats, goggles
- plastic containers and trays
- materials for labeling
- clipboards and pencils
- chalkboard and chalk for drawing diagrams and making presentations
- scales, rulers, measuring cups, and measuring spoons
- magnifying glasses, flashlights, and microscopes
- nonfiction reference books
- timer
- materials and specimens for study (these will depend on the goals of your program).

SETTING:

- Provide a table surrounded by chairs. Place this center near a water source. The materials and specimens will depend on your goals for your children.

ROLES AND VIEWPOINTS:

- How does a scientist answer questions about . . . ? What tools (including literacy materials) does a scientist need to make new discoveries?

- Tie science laboratory play to class inquiry themes. For example, if you are investigating insects, provide insect specimens, magnifying glasses, measurement utensils, materials for recording questions and making observations, nonfiction reference books on insects, clipboards, pencils, and laboratory coats.

SCHEDULING:

- Children may spontaneously engage in science laboratory play.
- Children may be scheduled to play in the science laboratory so that all have a chance to explore a specific concept.

Weather Station

SCHEMA BUILDING:

- View a videotaped weather report.
- Make a daily written record of the outside temperature and weather conditions with the children.
- Invite a weather professional to your classroom to give a 5–10 minute talk and show occupational materials. (Prepare interview questions in advance.)
- Tour a weather center.

MATERIALS:

- maps (state, country), weather maps
- pretend video camera
- pictures of weather with matching words (hot, cold, fair, snow, rain, sun, cloudy, partly cloudy, windy, thunder, lightning)
- notepad, markers, and tape
- pointer
- written weather reports and material for writing weather reports
- outdoor thermometer
- binoculars
- nonfiction reference books on weather

SETTING:

- Near a window with a outdoor thermometer, set up a magnetic chalkboard, a large message board, or a bulletin board with tacks. Provide a table or shelf for storing the materials listed above.
- Provide a pointer for reporting.

ROLES AND VIEWPOINTS:

- Who contributes to a weather report? What role does a television reporter play? How about a photographer? A meteorologist?
- What tools (including literacy materials) do these workers use to accomplish their jobs?
- Invite your children to tie weather station play to class inquiry themes. For example, if you are studying desert animals, invite your children to report on how weather affects these animals.

SCHEDULING:

- Children may spontaneously engage in weather station play.
- Children may be scheduled to attend the center in groups at set times. They may choose and try out a variety of roles.

References

Adcock, S. 1998. The Connection Between Home and School and Its Effect on Children's Writing. Action Research Project, Saginaw Valley State University, University Center, Michigan.

Adelman, C. 1992. "Play as a Quest for Vocation." *Journal of Curriculum Studies* 24 (2): 139–51.

Auerbach, E. 1995. "Which Way for Family Literacy: Intervention or Empowerment?" In *Family Literacy,* edited by L. Morrow, 11–27. Newark, DE: International Reading Association.

Barnes, D. 1993. "Supporting Exploratory Talk for Learning." In *Cycles of Meaning,* edited by K. M. Pierce and C. J. Gilles, 17–34. Portsmouth, NH: Heinemann.

Barr, R., and R. Johnson. 1997. *Teaching Reading and Writing in Elementary Classrooms.* White Plains, NY: Longman.

Bear, D., and D. Barone. 1998. *Developing Literacy.* Boston: Houghton Mifflin.

Berk, L., and A. Winsler. 1995. *Scaffolding Children's Learning: Vygotsky and Early Childhood Education.* Washington, DC: National Association for the Education of Young Children.

Bowman, B. 1994. "The Challenge of Diversity." *Phi Delta Kappan* 76 (3): 218–25.

Bredekamp, S., and C. Copple. 1997. *Developmentally Appropriate Practice in Early Childhood Programs.* Washington, DC: National Association for the Education of Young Children.

Bredekamp, S., and T. Rosegrant. 1992. *Reaching Potentials: Appropriate Curriculum and Assessment for Young Children.* Washington, DC: National Association for the Education of Young Children.

Brewer, J. 1992. *Early Childhood Education.* Needham Heights, MA: Allyn & Bacon.

Bruner, J. 1983. "Play, Thought, and Language." *Peabody Journal of Education* 60: 60–69.

Caswell, L., and N. Duke. 1998. "Non-Narrative as a Catalyst for Literacy Development." *Language Arts* 75 (2): 108–17.

Cazden, C. B. 1983. "Adult Assistance to Language Development: Scaffolds, Models and Direct Instruction." In *Developing Literacy,* edited by R. P. Parker and F. A. Davis, 3–17. Newark, DE: International Reading Association.

Clay, M. 1975. *What Did I Write?* Portsmouth, NH: Heinemann.

Davidson, J. 1996. *Emergent Literacy and Dramatic Play in Early Education.* Albany, NY: Delmar.

DeVries, R., and L. Kohlberg. 1987. *Constructivist Early Education: Overview and Comparison with Other Programs.* Washington, DC: National Association for the Education of Young Children.

Dewey, J. 1938. *Experience and Education.* New York: Macmillan.

Dyson, A. 1989. *Multiple Worlds of Child Writers.* New York: Teachers College Press.

Edwards, P. 1995. "Combining Parents' and Teachers' Thoughts About Storybook Reading at Home and School." In *Family Literacy,* edited by L. Morrow, 11–27. Newark, DE: International Reading Association.

Ferreiro, E. 1990. "Literacy Development: Psychogenesis." In *How Children Construct Literacy,* edited by Y. Goodman, 26–44. Newark, DE: International Reading Association.

Ferreiro, E., and A. Teberosky. 1982. *Literacy Before Schooling.* Translated by K. Castro. Portsmouth, NH: Heinemann.

Fountas, I., and G. Pinnell. 1996. *Guided Reading*. Portsmouth, NH: Heinemann.

Goodman, K. 1986. *What's Whole in Whole Language?* Portsmouth, NH: Heinemann.

———. 1996. *On Reading*. Portsmouth, NH: Heinemann.

Goodman, K., and Y. Goodman. 1990. "Vygotsky in a Whole Language Perspective." In *Vygotsky and Education*, edited by L. Moll, 223–50. Cambridge, MA: Cambridge University Press.

Goodman, Y. 1978. "Kidwatching: An Alternative to Testing." *National Elementary Principal* 57: 41–45.

———. 1980. "The Roots of Literacy." In *Claremont Reading Conference 44th Yearbook*, edited by M. P. Douglass. Claremont, CA: Claremont Reading Conference.

———. 1983. "Beginning Reading Development: Strategies and Principles." In *Developing Literacy*, edited by R. P. Parker and F. A. Davis, 68–83. Newark, DE: International Reading Association.

———. 1984. "The Development of Initial Literacy." In *Awakening to Literacy*, edited by H. Goelman, A. A. Oberg, and F. Smith. Portsmouth, NH: Heinemann.

Hall, N. 1998. "Young Children as Storytellers." In *Facilitating Preschool Literacy*, edited by R. Campbell, 84–99. Newark, DE: International Reading Association.

Halliday, M. 1975. *Learning How to Mean: Explorations in the Development of Language*. London: Edward Arnold.

Harste, J., C. Burke, and V. Woodward. 1981. *Children, Their Language and World: Initial Encounters with Print*. (Project NIE-G-79-0132). National Institute of Education.

Hay, J. 1994. "Distichs." In *Anthology of American Poetry*, edited by G. Gesner, 377–79. Avenel, NJ: Gramercy.

Hulit, L., and M. Howard. 1993. *Born to Talk*. New York: Macmillan.

International Reading Association and the National Association for the Education of Young Children (IRA/NAEYC). 1998. "Learning to Read and Write: Developmentally Appropriate Practices for Young Children." A Joint Position Statement. *Young Children* 53 (4): 30–54.

Isenberg, J. P., and M. R. Jalongo. 1997. *Creative Expression and Play in Early Childhood*. Upper Saddle River, NJ: Merrill.

Johnson, J. 1998. Family Literacy: Reciprocal Learning Between Home and School. Action Research Project, Saginaw Valley State University, University Center, Michigan.

Johnson, J., J. Christie, and T. Yawkey. 1987. *Play and Early Childhood Development*. Glenview, IL: Scott, Foresman and Company.

Kantor, R., S. Miller, and D. Fernie. 1992. "Diverse Paths to Literacy in a Preschool Classroom: A Sociocultural Perspective." *Reading Research Quarterly* 27 (3): 185–201.

King, C. 1998. Using Home-School Literature Experience Logs to Support Literacy Development in Kindergarten. Action Research Project, Saginaw Valley State University, University Center, Michigan.

Kostelnik, M., L. Stein, A. Whiren, and A. Soderman. 1993. *Guiding Children's Social Development*. Albany, NY: Delmar.

Linder, T. 1993. *Transdisciplinary Play-Based Intervention: Guidelines for Developing a Meaningful Curriculum for Young Children*. Baltimore: Paul H. Brookes.

Lindfors, J. 1991. *Children's Language and Learning*. Needham Heights, MA: Allyn and Bacon.

Lowman, L., and L. Ruhmann. 1998. "Simply Sensational Spaces: A Multi-'S' Approach to Toddler Environments." *Young Children* 58 (3): 11–17.

Martens, P., and Y. Goodman. 1996. "Invented Punctuation." In *Learning About Punctuation*, edited by N. Hall and A. Robinson, 37–53. Portsmouth, NH: Heinemann.

McCall, R. 1979. "Stages in Play Development Between Zero and Two Years of Age." In *Play and Learning,* edited by B. Sutton-Smith, 35–44. New York: Gardner Press.

McGee, L., and D. Richgels. 1996. *Literacy's Beginnings.* 2d edition. Needham Heights, MA: Allyn and Bacon.

Monighan-Nourot, P., B. Scales, J. Van Hoorn, and M. Almy. 1987. *Looking at Children's Play: A Bridge Between Theory and Practice.* New York: Teachers College Press.

Morrow, L. 1997. *The Literacy Center.* York, ME: Stenhouse.

Neuman, S., and K. Roskos. 1992. "Literacy Objects as Cultural Tools: Effects on Children's Literacy Behaviors in Play." *Reading Research Quarterly* 27 (3): 203–25.

———. 1993. *Language and Literacy Learning in the Early Years.* Orlando, FL: Harcourt Brace Jovanovich.

O'Reilly, A., and M. Bornstein. 1993. "Caregiver-Child Interaction in Play." In *The Role of Play in the Development of Thought,* edited by M. Bornstein and A. O'Reilly, 55–66. San Francisco: Jossey-Bass.

Pappas, C. C., and B. S. Pettigrew. 1998. "The Role of Genre in the Psycholinguistic Guessing Game of Reading." *Language Arts* 75 (1): 36–44.

Parten, M. 1932. "Social Participation Among Preschool Children." *Journal of Abnormal and Social Psychology* 27: 243–69.

Piaget, J. 1952. *The Construction of Reality in the Child.* New York: Basic Books.

———. 1962. *Play, Dreams and Imitation in Childhood.* New York: Norton.

———. 1973. *To Understand Is to Invent.* New York: Grossman.

Piaget, J., and B. Inhelder. 1969. *The Psychology of the Child.* New York: Basic Books.

Pierce, K. 1993. "Collaborative Curriculum Inquiry: Learning Through Evaluation." In *Cycles of Meaning,* edited by K. Pierce and C. Gilles, 293–314. Portsmouth, NH: Heinemann.

Pontecorvo, C., and C. Zucchermaglio. 1990. "A Passage to Literacy: Learning in a Social Context." In *How Children Construct Literacy,* edited by Y. Goodman, 59–98. Newark, DE: International Reading Association.

Raines, S., and R. Isbell. 1994. *Stories: Children's Literature in Early Education.* Albany, NY: Delmar.

Rosenblatt, L. 1991. "The Reading Transaction: What For?" In *Literacy in Process,* edited by B. M. Power and R. Hubbard, 114–27. Portsmouth, NH: Heinemann.

Roskos, K. 1995. "Creating Places for Play with Print." In *Readings for Linking Literacy and Play,* 8–17. Newark, DE: International Reading Association.

Roskos, K., C. Vukelich, J. Christie, B. Enz, and S. Neuman. 1995. *Linking Literacy and Play.* Newark, DE: International Reading Association.

Schrader, C. 1989. "Written Language Use Within the Context of Young Children's Symbolic Play." *Early Childhood Research Quarterly* 4: 225–44.

———. 1991. "Symbolic Play: A Source of Meaningful Engagements with Writing and Reading." In *Play and Early Literacy Development,* edited by J. Christie, 189–213. Albany: State University of New York.

Short, K., J. Harste, and C. Burke. 1996. *Creating Classrooms for Authors and Inquirers.* Portsmouth, NH: Heinemann.

Sowers, S. 1991. "Six Questions Teachers Ask About Invented Spelling." In *Literacy in Process,* edited by B. Miller and R. Hubbard. Portsmouth, NH: Heinemann.

Strickland, D., and M. Strickland. 1997. "Language and Literacy: The Poetry Connection." *Language Arts* 74 (3): 201–205.

Sulzby, E. 1985. "Children's Emergent Reading of Favorite Storybooks: A Developmental Study." *Reading Research Quarterly* 20: 458–81.

Taylor, D. 1983. *Family Literacy.* Portsmouth, NH: Heinemann.

Tracey, D. 1995. "Children Practicing Reading at Home: What We Know About How Parents Help." In *Family Literacy,* edited by L. Morrow. Newark, DE: International Reading Association.

Van Hoorn, J., P. Nourot, B. Scales, and K. Alward. 1993. *Play at the Center of the Curriculum.* New York: Merrill.

Vukelich, C. 1995. "Watch Me! Watch Me! Understanding Children's Literacy Knowledge." In *Readings for Linking Literacy and Play,* 23–33. Newark, DE: International Reading Association.

Vygotsky, L. 1978. *Mind in Society: The Development of Higher Psychological Processes,* edited and translated by M. Cole, V. John-Steiner, S. Scribner, and E. Souberman. Cambridge, MA: Harvard University Press.

Weaver, C. 1994. *Reading Process and Practice.* Portsmouth, NH: Heinemann.

Weinberger, J. 1998. "Young Children's Literacy Experiences Within the Fabric of Daily Life." In *Facilitating Preschool Literacy,* edited by R. Campbell, 39–50. Newark, DE: International Reading Association.

Whitmore, K., and Y. Goodman. 1995. "Transforming Curriculum in Language and Literacy." In *Reaching Potentials: Transforming Early Childhood Curriculum and Assessment,* Vol. 2, edited by S. Bredekamp and T. Rosegrant, 145–66. Washington, DC: National Association for the Education of Young Children.

Wilde, S. 1992. *You Ken Red This!* Portsmouth, NH: Heinemann.

BIBLIOGRAPHY OF CHILDREN'S BOOKS

Henkes, K. 1996. *Lilly's Purple Plastic Purse.* New York: Greenwillow Books.

Index